Enneagram and the Way of Jesus

Integrating Personality Theory with Spiritual Practices and Biblical Narratives

AJ Sherrill

ISBN: 153754103X
ISBN-13: 978-1537541037

Acknowledgements

Thank you to my wife, Elaina. You inspire me.

Thank you to my daughter, Eloise. You lighten me.

Thank you to my local community,
Trinity Grace Church Chelsea when the project began
and now Mars Hill Bible Church.
You put up with me.

I

Introduction:
The Challenge Of Discipleship

Obstacles to Discipleship

Discipleship is difficult. One would be hard pressed to present a generation where the demands of transformation into Christ's likeness have come with little effort. For the Christian, a holistically submitted life to God is a supernatural endeavor, yielding maturity in all areas of life. Whereas God is the transforming agent, formation does, in fact, require human effort. More often than not, the effort required runs counter-culture to the common societal worldview, which guides behavior at both conscious and subconscious levels.[1] Therefore, social imaginations are always influenced by competing agendas in culture. These agendas attempt to convert people to their version of the "good life."[2]

Following Jesus makes demands on the disciple's life. The history of the Church is replete with those whose bodily lives have been demanded, and for others, led to social exclusion. In the twentieth century, Dietrich Bonhoeffer reminded the Church that discipleship was costly. In the twenty-first century, it is inconvenient and often politically incorrect to follow a Jewish, non-credentialed rabbi who ostensibly was raised from the dead 2,000 years ago. No matter the era, discipleship always challenges natural human inclination, which tends toward self-reliance and self-preservation—from which Jesus came to save.

---

1   James K.A. Smith, *Desiring the Kingdom* (Grand Rapids, MI: Baker Academic, 2009), 80.
2   Ibid., 21.

New York Times columnist, David Brooks, rightly asserts, "Most of us have clearer strategies for how to achieve career success than we do for how to develop a profound character."[3] Brooks continues in his book, *The Road to Character*:

> We live in a society that encourages us to think about how to have a great career but leaves many of us inarticulate about how to cultivate the inner life. The competition to succeed and win admiration is so fierce that it becomes all-consuming. . . . We live in a culture that teaches us to promote and advertise ourselves and to master the skills required for success, but that gives little encouragement to humility, sympathy, and honest self-confrontation, which are necessary for building character. . . . Years pass and the deepest parts of yourself go unexplored and unstructured. You are busy, but you have a vague anxiety that your life has not achieved its ultimate meaning and significance.[4]

How tragic it is that Christians are little different than culture when it comes to inward growth. The Church must reengage Christians to prioritize their lives around becoming like Jesus. Among innumerable challenges to discipleship in the twenty-first century, urban West, three are salient: truth, time and transience.

Truth

The cynical question—what is truth—that Pilate put to Jesus, echoes throughout the ages. His inquiry captures the zeitgeist of the twenty-first century perhaps better than any other. In the postmodern West where relativism, subjectivism and existentialism here. reign supreme, calling a congregation beyond church attendance (which is a struggle in and of itself) and into radical, demanding spiritual formation is the difficult but imperative task. Perhaps

---

3   David Brooks, *The Road to Character* (New York: Random House, 2015) Kindle Edition, loc 92.
4   Ibid.

the greatest distinction between the world in which Jesus of Nazareth walked and the twenty-first century West is that Jesus' call to the original twelve disciples was within a milieu where Jewish monotheism, centered on objective truth claims, was generally a given. That age has passed. As a result, Christians today wrestle with the claim of one true path that governs the universe, one true Gospel story that is the meta-narrative of this world.

Imbibed in a narrative culture, subjective story often replaces objective truth. Postmodern sensibilities suggest that subjective story is most likely all there is, and that objective truth is either unknowable at best or illusory at worst. In this worldview, the individual's conscience becomes the standard of truth. Within this milieu, to assert the Gospel as the meta-narrative, under which all individual narratives find their meaning, can be perceived as oppressive. Therefore, Christian discipleship remains impossible for one who cannot get beyond individualism, and belief that the Gospel is a meta-narrative necessitating transformation on a personal level. The quest for truth matters.

Time

Time is another obstacle to Christians being formed in the twenty-first century. The problem with time is not that there are less hours in the day than in previous generations, nor is it that today's technology is inferior to attend to the day's tasks—just the opposite, actually. For all of the technological advances, most do not report an increase of margin. Further, one of the problems with many people's relationship to time is that there are more competing options for diversion than ever before. As Neil Postman rightly stated, humanity is increasingly "amusing ourselves to death." Where many have believed the aphorism, "time is money," greed, materialism and hedonism drive the idol many have made out of time. Henri Nouwen, the late Dutch author, defined spiritual discipline as "the effort to create some space in which God can act."[5] Creating space for

---

5   Henri Nouwen, "Moving from Solitude to Community to Ministry," *Leadership Journal* (Spring 1995): 81.

God within a culture immersed in social media, technological omnipresence and self-actualization makes discipleship a formidable task.

Today's world is polluted with noises unimaginable to previous generations. Recent research supports that noise pollution is on the rise. A study showed that in 1968 it took fifteen hours to record one hour of pure nature without the ambient sounds of airplanes, cars and other manufactured reverberations. As of the year 2005, it took more than 2,000 hours of recorded time to yield the same hour of pure nature sounds.[6] Another brand of distraction is interior noise. Although experienced differently, interior noise is often just as deafening as exterior noise. Most Millennial Christians in the urban West struggle to engage in uninterrupted time with anything. Relentlessly "checking in" with social media, email and entertainment has left scarce room for concerted effort in any area of life. In short, this is a time where most seek out interruptions for fear of missing out. Time is a significant challenge to twenty-first century discipleship.

Transience

The third challenge to discipleship—among many—is transience. According to economist Alan Blinder, Millenials can expect to change jobs four times before they are thirty years of age and ten times before they turn forty. Globalism continues to connect the world at a rate where few remain in the same geographic location for long periods of time, particularly between the ages of twenty-five and fifty years old.[7] Within this context commitment, accountability and covenant within a local body become low priorities for many Christians. One is tempted to suppose that, given the transient nature of life, commitment to a local church is unnecessary. Statistics report a decrease of transience as one ages. For example, one report claims:

---

6   Rob Bell, *Nooma: Noise* (Grand Rapids, MI: Zondervan), http://stmartins.co.za/documents/nooma/noise.pdf (accessed November 12, 2015).

7   Jon Zogby, "Employment 2.0: The Transient Age," Forbes Magazine, http://www.forbes.com/2009/09/09/temporary-employment-new-job-opinions-columnists-john-zogby.html (accessed November 12, 2015).

Because there are so many Americans, even a small percentage represents a large quantity of people. If you consider a move outside of the same county a "long-distance" move—there are 17 million annual long-distance moves, with over a million of these moves outside the country. The major new move activity takes place within the 18-34 year olds, with people in their 20s representing the highest concentration. Once people reach their 50s, their move rate is minimal. And in people over the age of 70, the move percentages are below 2 percent annually.[8]

It is clear the greatest challenge to discipleship, with regard to transience, is emerging generations. And even when one chooses to remain in the same place, it is rare that one's support group will remain with them. Over the span of several decades, transience is often a tremendous obstacle to formation.

Discipleship and the Enneagram

The aforementioned obstacles to discipleship in the twenty-first century can feel insurmountable. The following pages attempt to unfold a pathway for those who desire to subvert the cultural milieu and take formation into the image of Jesus seriously. Spiritual formation is a lifelong pursuit. Although there are moments of profound, instantaneous breakthrough, most spiritual formation is incremental, resulting from a long commitment to practices. This work uses the terms "practices" and "disciplines" interchangeably, which are simply commitments to specific tasks and rhythms for the purpose of formation. Disciplines are not always enjoyable and seldom bear immediate fruit. However, a commitment to disciplines over a long period of time yields growth, often referred to as spiritual maturity, transformation or sanctification.

The pressing issue this work seeks to address is that of

8   David Bancroft Avrick, "How Many People Move Each Year – and Who Are They?" Melissa Data, http://www.melissadata.com/enews/articles/0705b/1.htm (accessed November 12, 2015).

maturity in the midst of the aforementioned challenges. Further, an over-simplified discipleship is often employed in many local churches. Humans are diverse. This is evident by their appetites, preferences, genetics and personalities. Therefore, if humans are diverse, the local church should aim to embody spiritual formation with human diversity in mind.

The Enneagram is a theory of personality that exposes weaknesses as much as it celebrates strengths. Suggesting there are nine personality types in the world, the Enneagram reveals core motivations as to why people do the things that they do. In short, it can be used as a tool to reveal one's barriers to Christ-likeness. For each personality this work will prescribe specific practices for engagement in order to form deeper Christ-likeness over the course of time. To be certain, all spiritual disciplines are helpful no matter one's personality. However, due to the amount of practices that have been developed throughout the centuries, the reader is encouraged to locate their Enneagram type and then engage practices that will come naturally (referred to as "downstream disciplines") and unnaturally (referred to as "upstream disciplines"). Both downstream and upstream disciplines are important for the purpose of holistic formation.

PART ONE

The Enneagram
Personality Theory

1

A HISTORY OF THE ENNEAGRAM

The Enneagram is a personality theory comprised of nine different types. Derived from the Greek language, it means "nine (ennea) diagram." Some refer to the theory as the "faces of the soul," and attach its origins to Pythagorus due to mathematical speculation.[9] However, the origins of the theory are largely unknown as this work will present. The gift of this personality theory is self-knowledge. With self-knowledge one becomes self-aware, opening exploration for transformative growth.

The Enneagram provides both good and bad news. The good news is that, like other personality theories, it provides feedback apropos to one's strengths. This can often serve as a reinforcement of what one already is already aware of. The Enneagram is also often perceived as bad news because it provides feedback regarding one's weaknesses. Conditioned at a young age to hone in on strengths, many are prone to ignore weaknesses. Thus, some traditions such as Buddhism aver that spirituality is a matter of "waking up," or coming to terms with what is so that one can confront reality and transcend brokenness. Christians refer to this as transforming the sin nature. Before delving into the "where" and the "who" of Enneagram origins, it is important to first understand the "why."

According to Enneagram expert, Sandra Maitri, "The nine ennea-types arise out of reaction to the loss of our basic trust and concomitant disconnection from being."[10] From a Christian per-

---

9   Don Richard Riso and Russ Hudson, Personality Types: *Using the Enneagram for Self-Discovery* (Boston: Houghton Mifflin Harcourt, 1996), Kindle Edition, loc 376.

10   Sandra Maitri, *The Enneagram of Passions and Virtues: Finding the Way Home* (New York: Penguin Publishing Group, 2005), Kindle Edition, loc 30.

spective, this failure to trust and experience of disconnection in any given environment stems from the fall of creation recorded in Genesis 3. Because of the fall, the human race seeks to hold situations in various ways to restabilize their world. One can understand these "holdings" as strategies to cope, manage and succeed in life. A.H. Almas, Kuwaiti author and spiritual teacher, relates to the Enneagram as a tool that "maps the various ways the ego develops to deal with the absence, disruptions, ruptures, and discontinuities of holding."[11] He articulates the holdings of each type in the following way:

Type One: Triumphing over the Fall through self-improvement

Type Two: Manipulating the way others perceive them through service

Type Three: Developing oneself to make success happen

Type Four: Denying any disconnection with self, but trying to control it

Type Five: Isolating oneself through withdraw and avoidance

Type Six: Fearfully paranoid about the dangers in an environment

Type Seven: Avoiding the pain of disconnection through seeking pleasure

Type Eight: Angry at the Fall, they fight for justice and revenge

Type Nine: Make everything better by submitting through routine living[12]

---

11   A. H. Almaas, *Facets of Unity: The Enneagram of Holy Ideas* (Berkeley, CA: Diamond Books, 1998), 44-45.
12   Ibid.

The idea is that "ordinary experience is filtered through the veils of personality."[13] See appendix A for a diagram of the nine types.

The personality mostly is the egoic self that has been cultivated through years of reacting and responding to life events. Don Richard Riso believes the "personality is a form of defense that we have continued to use for reasons that started in our infancy."[14] Maitri explains it:

> As we develop a personality structure in early childhood, we gradually lose contact with Being. By the time our psychological structure is solidified, our contact with the depth of ourselves is largely lost to our consciousness. The Enneagram of personality dominates our experience. With the loss of experiential contact with what makes life full, rich, and meaningful—our deepest nature—our personality has at its core a gaping absence.[15]

As people grow, the idea is that they maintain personality, but do not over-identify with it. People are able to stand outside of themselves in self-awareness to perceive themselves in situations and adjust accordingly.

Whereas many contemporary personality theories galvanize strengths, the Enneagram does not aim at building the ego. Rather, it aims to aid learning in beginning to let go of what is unnecessary. Thomas Merton referred to this unnecessary way of being as the "false self." One must be careful, then, to not misunderstand this. The Enneagram does not hope to expose the strategies of one's personality in order to lose personality. However, it helps to name what is often hidden to each person, and once named the person can then seek transformation for the broken areas that manifest from their personality. Outlining the basis of why the Enneagram developed and proliferated, the "what" and "where" of its origin is important.

---

13 Maitri, *The Enneagram of Passions and Virtues*, 1.
14 Don Richard Riso and Russ Hudson, *Understanding the Enneagram: The Practical Guide to Personality Types* (Boston: Houghton Mifflin Harcourt, 2000), Kindle Edition, loc 183.
15 Maitri, *The Enneagram of Passions and Virtues*, 2.

The Origins and Purpose of the Enneagram

The exact origin of the Enneagram is mysterious. The original conceiver(s) is largely thought to be unknown. Whereas many historians and authors espouse it first surfaced among the Sufis, others surmise that it originated in the third century B.C. somewhere in the Middle East. These are speculations at best.[16] Riso and Hudson, Christian critics of the theory, which are discussed in detail at the end of this chapter, are surprised to find:

> More likely sources of the system can be traced to early teachings in the Judeo-Christian tradition and in early Greek philosophy. The symbol itself, with its fascinating geometry and its basis in the mathematics of ratio and proportion, strongly suggests Greek roots, particularly the teachings of Pythagoras, the founder of a philosophical school which flourished in the fourth and fifth centuries B.C. Oscar Ichazo, the inventor of the modern Enneagram, supports this view of the Enneagram's lineage. . . . The first and most important source of the types comes from the idea of the Seven Deadly Sins, with the addition of two other "sins" to bring the total to nine. The seven deadly sins, which include pride, envy, anger, gluttony, avarice, lust, and sloth, were part of the teachings of medieval Christianity, and were studied and commented on extensively throughout Europe.[17]

Although its origins may be debatable, what is important is the usefulness of the theory.[18] If the Desert Fathers of the Christian Tradition found the contents that now make up the modern Enneagram useful, and not inherently Satanic or cultish, today, Christians should not hastily discredit its veracity before first examining its fruit.

---

16 Riso and Hudson, Personality Types, locs 358-362.
17 Ibid., locs 394-398.
18 See appendix B for a diagram that aggregates the general consensus, if there is one, surrounding its origins.

Thus far the why, where and who of the Enneagram has surfaced. Turning attention to the "what," the structure of the Enneagram is both peculiar and insightful. Refer to appendices C through F for corresponding images of its structure. As previously stated and shown in Appendix A, the personality types are appointed numbers. From the onset it is helpful for the learner to know that numbers do not express types with a view toward numerical rankings. There is no significance to one type being any better or worse than another based on the number. The numbers distinguish one type from another, and each Type contains both strengths and weaknesses. For a more robust understanding of the root sins for each Type, avoidance strategies and pitfalls, refer to Appendices C through E.

Beyond the nine types, it is now helpful to comprehend what is referred to as "triads." This will become important to understand in Chapter 3 as one seeks practices for transformative impact based on type. Concerning triads, Riso and Hudson state succinctly (refer to appendix F for a corresponding image):

> The Enneagram is an arrangement of nine personality types in three Triads. There are three personality types in the Feeling Triad, three in the Thinking Triad, and three in the Instinctive Triad. Each Triad consists of three personality types which are best characterized by the assets and liabilities of that Triad. For example, personality type Two has particular strengths and liabilities involving its feelings, which is why it is one of the three types in the Feeling Triad. The Seven's assets and liabilities involve thinking, which is why it is in the Thinking Triad, and so forth for all nine personality types.[19]

In Appendix G one may also note the common tendencies based on triad for each type. These are tendencies each type within

---

19   Riso and Hudson, *Personality Types*, locs 610-614.

one of the three triads tends toward when unhealthy. Appendix H shows how triads play out in the social sphere. Finally, Appendix I reveals the focus on each type within triads as it relates to its fixation in life. For example, Nine's core fixation is self-forgetfulness, as Eights and Ones can do this too. Three's core fixation is image, where Twos and Fours also struggle in this area. Six's core fixation is fear, where Fives and Sevens dwell there as well. Although each type wrestles with self-forgetfulness, image and fear, some types reside there more thoroughly than others. Another way to put it is that within each triad, the types are motivated primarily by self-forgetfulness, image or fear.

Like an onion, there are layers upon layers to discover in the Enneagram. This work will not delve into the depths of what are referred to as "wings" or where one goes in stress and security based on the shapes within the circle (triangle and hexagon). For an in depth analysis on its structure, refer to Riso and Hudson's seminal work, *Personality Types: Using the Enneagram for Self-Discovery*, and Richard Rohr and Andreas Eberts's, *The Enneagram: A Christian Perspective*.

Twentieth Century Re-emergence and Scientific Basis

Although the origin of the Enneagram remains somewhat mysterious, its twentieth century re-emergence is cogent. Born in Armenia, George Ivanovich Gurdjieff, a spiritual teacher and adventure seeker, brought the Enneagram West, having learned versions of it from Eastern Orthodox and Sufi influences.[20] When Oscar Ichazo, founder of the Arica School, learned various forms of the Enneagram, it is believed that he synthesized it into the form of what is commonly used today. According to Riso and Hudson,

> The modern Enneagram, therefore, seems to be the result of Ichazo's brilliant synthesis of a number of related systems of thought about the nature and structure of human consciousness, brought together in the enigmatic Ennea-

---

20   Ibid., locs, 411-412.

gram symbol. It is best described as a contemporary and evolving theory of human nature based on a variety of time-honored sources and traditions. At the same time, it is quite clear that there is no single body of knowledge, no continuous "oral tradition" of the Enneagram handed down from antiquity. Rather, many traditions and innovations, both modern and ancient, have gone into the creation of this remarkable system.[21]

Intersecting with Claudio Naranjo, a Chilean-born psychiatrist, Ichazo and Naranjo brought it to Berkley, California where Naranjo employed it through his practice. It was then proliferated through various Enneagram workshops where, "in the early 1970s, several American Jesuit priests—most notably the Reverend Robert Ochs, S.J.—learned the material from Claudio Naranjo. Ochs taught it to other Jesuits at Loyola University in Chicago, and from there it spread quickly."[22]

Arguments for and Against its Use in Christian Formation

Christian opponents of the Enneagram are rife due to its speculative origins, disputed psychology and universal application. Whereas some critiques are understandable, many are not compelling. A primary example of its questionable science can be traced back to recent critiques in 2004, where the US Conference of Catholic Bishops' Committee on Doctrine released a report against the credibility of the tool as a viable instrument of scientific psychology. In it, the report concluded:

> An examination of the origins of Enneagram teaching reveals that it does not have credibility as an instrument of scientific psychology and that the philosophical and religious ideas of its creators are out of keeping with basic elements of Christian faith on several points. Conse-

---

21 Ibid., locs, 474-479.
22 Ibid., locs, 511-515.

quently, the attempt to adapt the Enneagram to Christianity as a tool for personal spiritual development shows little promise of providing substantial benefit to the Christian community.[23]

The Catholic World Report further claimed the theory "encourages unhealthy self-absorption."[24] Whereas this may be true in some cases, one need not undermine a personality theory simply because learners of that theory abuse it. If that were the case, every personality theory should be dismissed as well. To the contrary, the Enneagram is designed to increase one's self-awareness toward transformation rather than self-absorption. In the same article, the author suggests a relativizing of sin so that one blames the Type rather than taking personal responsibility. This argument is unfounded as the person is complicit when they play into the default behaviors of their Type. Benedictine Sister and author on the Enneagram, Suzanne Zuercher, allayed fears of relativizing sin as an inevitable consequence of the theory in stating, "If you know the Enneagram, it states in numerous ways that our greatest sinfulness comes from our desire to redeem ourselves."[25] Therefore, it does not relativize personal responsibility, but rather places it on the person within the type, and aims to inspire the learner to seek transformation.

Mark Scandrette, author and adjunct professor at Fuller Theological Seminary, believes that although the Enneagram has been scientifically validated by the objective assessment firm, SLH Group PLC, it needs no validation because it is "self-verifying through experience."[26] He believes it should only be viewed as a tool for personal transformation to avoid using it maliciously to "shrink others down."[27] Finally, Scandrette claims much of the crit-

23 US Bishops' Secretariat for Doctrine and Pastoral Practices, "A Brief Report on the Origins of the Enneagram," *New York Catholic Reporter*, http://natcath.org/NCR_Online/documents/ennea2.htm (accessed September 10, 2015).
24 Anna Abbott, "A Dangerous Practice," *The Catholic World Report*, http://www. catholicworldreport.com/Item/994/a_dangerous_practice.aspx (accessed September 10, 2015).
25 Ibid.
26 Mark Scandrette, phone interview by author, August 5, 2015, New York.
27 Ibid.

icism by the Christian Church in recent years is due to its acceptance in New Age communities.

Another common objection to the trustworthiness of the Enneagram for Christian formation is that it "gives rise to a deterministic mindset at odds with Christian freedom."[28] To the contrary, the Enneagram helps identify areas of weakness, which, for the Christian, assists self-awareness for the purpose of greater transformation into the image of Christ through the Spirit's leading in spiritual practices and community. For the Christian it is particularly useful because it helps expose personal brokenness, sin and shame, which can provide necessary clarity toward transformation. Maitri avers, "The Enneagram's deeper function is to point the way to who we are beyond the level of the personality, a dimension of ourselves that is infinitely more profound, more interesting, more rewarding, and more real."[29] Thinkers such as Maitri and Scandrette view the Enneagram through the lens of transformative *telos* rather than an end in and of itself.

Still others protest it to be a new form of Gnosticism. This has arisen due to numerology, which Deuteronomy 18:10-14 ostensibly forbids. Proponents of this view assert the Enneagram masquerades as a secret contact with divine energy and relationship with God rather than faith in the death and resurrection of Jesus.[30] Father William Meninger of St. Benedict's Monastery in Snowmass, Colorado conducts retreats on the Enneagram and the Centering Prayer. He offered the following as a response to critics: "The Enneagram teaches self-knowledge. . . . Self-knowledge is the virtue of humility. Humility is the primary virtue. Self-knowledge is important to the spiritual journey. [The Enneagram] is only a tool."[31] The argument that the Enneagram is a form of new Gnosticism is easily refuted because, unlike first and second century Gnosticism, there

---

28   Ibid.
29   Sandra Maitri, *The Spiritual Dimension of the Enneagram: Nine Faces of the Soul* (New York: Penguin Publishing Group, 2000), Kindle Edition, loc page 3.
30   Ibid.
31   Ibid.

17

is no promise of salvation within understanding the theory.[32] Rather, one utilizes self-knowledge in order to pursue God (via spiritual practices as this work will show) for transformation. The Enneagram is a useful tool employed to understand one's motives more clearly and then move toward transformation. It is a personality theory.

It is true that some have twisted its contents into a form a religion. However, if one regards its contents complicit with Gnosticism, one must also regard other personality theories such as Myers-Briggs, Strengths-Finders and others in the same way. Finally, opponents must concede that the Desert Fathers employed much of the contents of the Enneagram, implicit and explicit. Riso and Hudson affirm its Christian historicity as the "nine passions are based on the seven deadly sins, with two more passions bringing the total to nine. The One's passion is Anger, the Two's is Pride, the Four's is Envy, the Five's is Avarice, the Seven's is Gluttony, the Eight's is Lust, and the Nine's is Sloth. To type Three, he assigned the passion of Deceit, and to type Six, that of Fear."[33] Even as early as the fourth century, Augustine of Hippo "wrote that wherever truth is found, it belongs to God."[34]

A Christian Perspective

Seldom does one read of Christians critiquing the Magi for the knowledge they attained that led them across the wilderness by a star to find the Christ child born in Bethlehem. In fact, this narrative is affirmed by Catholic, Orthodox and Anglican churches year after year. It should not, then, surprise Christians to find God revealing through means such as the Enneagram whose learners are wider than the great Christian traditions. Few are critical of Paul for integrating the tomb of the unknown God in Acts 17 in order to spur his listeners on to accept the claims of the Gospel.

---

32   John Flader, "Enneagram is not Recommended," *The Catholic Leader,* http://catholicleader.com.au/analysis/Enneagram-is-not-recommended (accessed November 12, 2015).

33   Riso and Hudson, *Personality Types,* locs 481-483.

34   Diane Tolomeo, Pearl Gervais and Remi De Roo, *Biblical Characters and the Enneagram: Images of Transformation* (Victoria, BC: Newport Bay Publishing, 2001), ix.

The Enneagram, too, is like the revelation to the Magi, or the tomb of the unknown God that can be employed to call people into transformation in Christ. Scandrette believes, the "Enneagram reveals our false scripts. I am prone to believe things that are exaggerated or untrue. I am prone to believe the lies that I am the sum of my achievements, appearance, or uniqueness. I am prone to hide myself from others because the world is scary."[35] In his work on the Enneagram, Rohr contributes, "The gift that the Enneagram gives is self-knowledge or self-awareness. With self-knowledge, the individual can move into pursuing inner-work, which is often painful." [36]Given that much of the New Testament Epistles are dedicated to the need of ongoing sanctification, the Enneagram is one of the best tools in the twenty-first century for Christians to take seriously their journey of life transformation. The Enneagram is a theory yielding self-awareness. It provides a window into one's own self so that one may peer within their motivations for life. With this critical self-understanding one then can orient daily practices and regular rhythms with the possibility of transformation into Christ-likeness.

It is important to note that the aim is not to rid personality. Rather it is to be transformed within personality so that one becomes aware of defaulting to actions of the sin nature. Riso rightly concludes, "People do not change from one basic personality type to another. Each person is a unique individual within that larger group and, in the last analysis, remains that type for the rest of his or her life. In reality, people do change in many ways throughout their lives, but their basic personality type does not change."[37] Riso claims that there are three stages of work one must undergo to experience deep transformation: "First, we need to learn self-observation so that we can see our behavior as objectively as possible. Second, we need to increase our self-understanding so that we can know the true motives for our behavior. And third, we need to cultivate awareness or presence, which facilitates and deepens the process of

35 Scandrette, phone interview.
36 Richard Rohr, Andreas Ebert and Peter Heinegg, *The Enneagram: A Christian Perspective* (New York: Crossroad Pub, 2001), xi.
37 Riso and Hudson, *Personality Types*, locs 658-660.

transformation."[38] The goal, then, is for the learner to understand his personality and then grow into health within it.

For decades, the debate about nature versus nurture concerning personality has raged. Maitri claims, "An interesting question arises: does our view of reality shape the way we feel, or is it the other way around?[39] This is another way of asking which is more primary to the formation of our personality structure: the loss of perception of reality as it is, or the loss of the felt connection with the realm of Being? Does the passion give rise to the fixation, or is it the other way around?" To this debate, this work suggests humans are born with genetic proclivities (nature). However, through the course of life experiences they solidify personality roughly by the age of twenty (nurture). For example, one may have the genetic proclivity of a Three, Seven or Eight (all part of the assertive type category, as detailed below). However, over the course of time, one's life experiences and responses to those experiences solidify personality. Rohr asserts that First World Countries are replete with certain personality types (Threes, for instance) that one would find far less of in Third World Countries.[40] This is due to the fact that societies nurture genetic proclivities into solidified personalities. Succinctly put, personality may begin with genetics, but is developed over the course of life experience.

Many refer to the second half of the twentieth century as the psychological century.[41] Whereas psychology is important, the aim of this work is spiritual. The implications of the Enneagram are social, spiritual and psychological. Therefore, to focus entirely on the psychological dimensions of the theory lacks the transformational thrust that this work aims to achieve. Whereas the Enneagram can be utilized to reveal sin (both inherent and personal), when paired with spiritual practices over the course of a lifetime, one can grow into the image of Jesus through the work of the Holy Spirit. To that end this work journeys forward.

---

38 Riso and Hudson, Understanding the Enneagram, locs 186-188.
39 Maitri, *The Enneagram of Passions and Virtues*, loc page 3.
40 Rohr, Ebert and Heinegg, *The Enneagram*, 89.
41 Maitri, *The Enneagram of Passions and Virtues*, loc 158.

2

THE ENNEAGRAM PERSONALITY TYPES

Determining Your Type

Most personality theories locate an individual's classification through testing. However, Enneagram expert and veteran teacher, Suzanne Stabile, believes one does not really find her type as much as the type finds her. She asserts the most accurate way to assess one's Enneagram type is to first understand each one. The type that best reflects one's personality will ultimately emerge as that person reads because it is the one that causes the greatest humiliation while reading the descriptions.

Humiliation is experienced as the "type finds us" because hidden in the subconscious, one knows his impact in the world. Whereas people can and do make helpful contributions in this world, they are also vaguely aware that they cause rupture as well. From exploitation and rage, to passive-aggression and fear, humanity is riddled with internal brokenness that is often externally transmitted toward others. Like stained glass, when light passes through, the image can be beautiful. However, the first step toward wholeness is recognizing the fact that all are broken and fragmented, needing to be placed back into a cohesive whole in order to reclaim the identity that God has for all humanity through grace.

It is true that each person manifests each type in various ways. People are not homogenous creatures that can simply be reduced to a type to explain the totality of their existence. However, everyone resides within one core personality more than the others. This is the starting place to discovering one's uniqueness. Maitri suggests,

Figuring out what your ennea-type is can be a tricky matter. Some people recognize their type immediately by reading or hearing the descriptions; some people's type is obvious to one who knows the Enneagram by looking at them, while others are more difficult for themselves or anyone else to type. Why one's type is clear-cut with some people and indiscernible with others seems to be one of those mysteries about the Enneagram and the soul.[42]

Whereas some locate their type using questionnaires and inventories, Ichazo used facial characteristics, believing specific regions of the face correspond with types.[43] Most suggest beginning with a test as an introduction, then reading the full descriptions for confirmation or rejection of the test results. Below are summary (not exhaustive) descriptions that help the inquirer to focus in on one or two possibilities while eliminating others. Therefore, one should begin with a test,[44] then read the descriptions below, and, finally, seek further analysis from the resources located in the appendices. If, after all this, there is still a struggle to discern a type one should think back to who she was at age twenty, and how she was motivated toward action. Rohr believes around that age people live most evidently from their core personality.[45]

Maitri warns of mistyping as a common occurrence. To avoid this, first, the inquirer should seek and find their type. Informing another who they are can be both dangerous and robs the inquirer from making the discovery. Therefore, let the inquirer be on his own journey of personality discovery rather than diagnosing him, especially since that inquirer is the only human on the planet with access to his interiority. Second, when one finds difficulty in determining type, Maitri suggests, "determining a corner" to narrow the options down.[46] For example, the three dominant corners of the nine personalities are fear, image and self-forgetting.

42 Maitri, *The Spiritual Dimension of the Enneagram*, loc 470.
43 Ibid.
44 Such as this free one online made available by the Enneagram Institute: https://www.Enneagraminstitute.com/rheti-sampler/.
45 Rohr, Ebert and Heinegg, *The Enneagram*, 41.
46 Maitri, *The Spiritual Dimension of the Enneagram*, loc 470.

Figure 1. The Enneagram

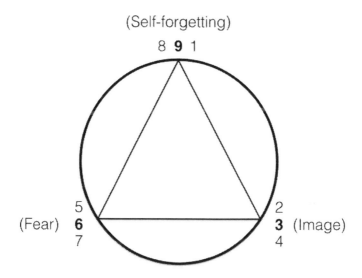

If the inquirer belongs to the Five, Six, Seven corner, motivating factors in life are fear based. If the inquirer belongs to the Two, Three, Four corner, motivating factors are image based. A person in this corner is often concerned with their presentation and what others perceive about them. Finally, if the inquirer belongs to the Eight, Nine, One corner, motivating factors are self-forgetfulness, which means that his attention is outward focused. Again, every human experiences all of these motives. However, one is seeking to locate within one primary corner from which much of life is lived. Determining a corner is not essential to discovering one's type. However, for those having difficulty it is a great tool for refinement.

Riso, author and expert teacher on the Enneagram, offers several key points of understanding as one delves into the personality theory:

> First, people do not change from one basic personality type to another. . . . In reality, people do change in many ways throughout their lives, but their basic personality type does not change. Second, the descriptions of the

personality types are universal and apply equally to males and females. . . . Third, not everything in the description of your basic type will apply to you all the time. Fourth, as we have seen, the Enneagram uses numbers to designate each of the personality types . . . the numbers are value neutral. No one number is better or worse than any other number.[47]

Each of these points is helpful as one endeavors in the process of personality discovery. The personality is like of an onion being peeled back layer after layer. Much of life remains personally mysterious. Over the course of a lifetime the personality solidifies as one lives from it. People act and do not realize it, they live in default mode, and what they think is typical behavior is often muscle memory to each person. Learning one's personality helps to gain perspective on life, diagnose how one "ticks," and also provides clarity as to how others perceive her. The Enneagram personality theory is both basic to understand and complex to fully comprehend. Due to the limitations of this work, the focus on the Enneagram theory will be simple, utilized with the intent to offer spiritual practices to better conform the Christian into the image of Jesus.

---

47   Riso and Hudson, *Personality Types*, locs 660-661.

Type One

ONE WORD: Perfectionist

FOUR WORDS: Idealist, Principled, Independent, Critical

SURVIVAL STRATEGY: I must be perfect and good.

FAMOUS ONES: Ralph Waldo Emerson, Mary Poppins, Martin Luther, George Bernard Shaw[48]

According to Riso, Ones are located in the Relating Triad.[49] They need to feel justified by the conscience before they can act. Ones struggle to relate to their environment because of the incessant need for perfection before acting. They are dissatisfied with the way the world currently is, and seek an idealized state. Extremely principled with strong convictions, they are also dissatisfied with their own imperfection within the imperfect world, and live toward the way things "ought" to be. Simultaneously, they fear making a mistake, which often leaves them immobile. Average Ones become angry and frustrated easily when their surrounding environment does not cooperate with their standard of perfection and processes.[50]

From an early age Ones learned to behave properly.[51] They often recall being painfully criticized. As a result, they learned to monitor themselves to avoid mistakes that would come to other's attention. Mirroring the Puritans, they work hard, are independent and often self-righteous.[52] They are convinced that life is hard and that ease is earned. They understand delayed-gratification better than any other Type. Often their natural desires were forbidden as children so they block desire to do the right thing. Severely compulsive, they believe there is always room for improvement. They are critical, but procrastinate out of fear of getting it wrong or making a mistake.

48 Helen Palmer, *The Enneagram: Understanding Yourself and the Others in Your Life* (San Francisco: Harper Collins, 1991), 94.
49 Don Richard Riso, *Discovering Your Personality Type: The New Enneagram Questionnaire* (Boston: Houghton Mifflin Co, 1995), 78.
50 Ibid.
51 Palmer, *The Enneagram*, 72-73.
52 Ibid., 73.

Often good teachers, Ones strive to set healthy examples of the way things "ought" to be. They are often model children who are motivated to "be good," "try harder" and "get it right." Morally, behaviorally and vocationally they are eternally dissatisfied with the current state. From an early age they sought perfection out of fear of losing the love of their dear ones. They are often gifted children and are later viewed as "anal retentive." It is a heavy thing to be a One because they are relentlessly embattled in inner trials. They chase discounts, clean rooms, are committed to duty and disappoint themselves by their own imperfection. This often leads them to an inner anger.[53]

Certainly, being a One is a burden.[54] Ones often repress anger because the world (and themselves) is not what it should be. They see through idealized glasses. They are desperate to be correct and right. They suffer from a relentless inner critic. When they are criticized it is severe for them because it reinforces their inner critic. They are good at perfecting things when the world is not going well. When they experience a situation that is out of their control (for example, if a loved one is sick) they clean their house from the need to perfect something within their realm of control. They best operate from within strict, clear guidelines, feedback and a single course of action.[55] They suppress anger so that when it does surface it is usually related to something deeper.

The lie Ones believe: "It's not ok to make a mistake."
The truth Ones need: "You are good."[56]

Type Two
ONE WORD: Helper

FOUR WORDS: Relational, Generous, Insecure, Self-unaware

SURVIVAL STRATEGY: I must be helpful and caring.

FAMOUS TWOS: Madonna, Elizabeth Taylor, Dolly Parton, Elvis Presley[57]

---

53   Rohr, Ebert and Heinegg, *The Enneagram*, 49.
54   Suzanne Stabile, class lecture, *Know Your Number*, Christ Church-Greenwich, March 21, 2015.
55   Ibid.
56   Ibid.
57   Palmer, *The Enneagram*, 124.

Service is very important to Twos. At their best, Twos are healing presences in the world.[58] They move toward others, but are often, subconsciously, motivated by self-interest. Further, they rarely notice their own insecurity when doing this because they are self-unaware. The average Two talks more about serving others than actually serving others. Palmer says, "They are marked by the need for affection and approval; they want to be loved, protected and feel important in other's lives."[59] They develop keen perception to discern the moods and preferences of others and then act accordingly. Twos easily alter their own tastes and preferences to serve the desires of others. This gives rise to what Palmer calls the "multiple self."[60] They can be characterized as so in tune with the feelings of others that they lose touch with their own feelings. Over time, this can lead to Twos having difficulty discerning personal longings and preferences.

"Twos have an exaggerated need for validation."[61] They are prone to flattery and giving public approval of others for personal purposes. Some Twos report that early in life they had to provide care and support for both older and younger members of the family. Because of this, they develop a "need to be needed" which results in secret pride. Whereas they are extremely helpful, they expect (often demand) gratitude in return. Caricatures of this type include the "Jewish mother," and the "pastor's wife."[62]

At the root, immature Twos struggle with identity, which is why they invest their resources into others, hoping their acknowledgment and gratitude will fill the void. Describing how immature Twos are prone to function in committed relationships, Helen Palmer claims:

> The early phases of a relationship are dominated by a Two living out those aspects that will flatter the partner's needs. The later phases of a relationship are dominat-

58   Riso, *Discovering Your Personality Type*, 66.
59   Palmer, *The Enneagram*, 101.
60   Ibid., 105.
61   Rohr, Ebert and Heinegg, *The Enneagram*, 63.
62   Ibid.

ed by the feelings of being controlled by the partner's will, coupled by an overwhelming desire for freedom. . . . Twos experience a conflict between the habit of molding self-presentation so as to be ultimately irresistible to a partner and wanting the freedom to do whatever they please.[63]

In the end, Twos gain control through helpfulness. They also believe others need them in order to thrive. However, they often want recognition of their usefulness, lest they become insecure and angry. Their twin preoccupations are gaining approval and avoiding rejection. They take subversive pride in their assistance to the extent that they hope others will not be able to get along without them. Twos are other-oriented to the point that if they are not needed, they believe themselves to be unwanted. Questions Twos should ask themselves before serving others: What is my agenda? What is the return? Does this person want my help?

The lie Twos believe: "It's not ok to have my own needs."
The truth Twos need: "You are wanted."

Type Three

ONE WORD: Achiever

FOUR WORDS: Image-conscious, Ambitious, Adaptable, Motivated

SURVIVAL STRATEGY: I must be impressive and attractive.

FAMOUS THREES: Ronald Reagan, Farrah Fawcett, Walt Disney, John F. Kennedy[64]

The axiom of the Three is to avoid failure and maximize success. They are often out of touch with their feelings. Adept in agility, they can adapt to whatever is needed in the moment to ensure success, security and social assimilation. Above all, they seek

---

63   Palmer, *The Enneagram*, 102.
64   Ibid., 154.

to project a desirable image.[65]   Unlike Twos who ask, "Do you like me?" the Three asks, "Am I successful?"[66]   As children, Threes were prized for their achievements. Thus, their proclivities are seldom genetic, but are learned from and reinforced by guardians. Threes recall feeling worth through performance and image rather than through emotional and social connectedness. Palmer states, "Because they were loved for their achievements, they learned to suspend their own emotions and focus their attention on earning the status that would guarantee them love. It was very important to avoid failure, because only winners were worthy of love."[67]

Threes are driven by "3 C's:" Competency, Comparison and Competition. They are some of the most competent people in their respective fields because identity hangs in the balance. Whereas they work hard to develop competence, on-lookers often would not know because Threes give the appearance of ease. They ardently compare themselves with others at the office in order to gauge their skill and expertise. Last, they compete to be first, to get the promotion or receive whatever award is available in order to feel worthy within their environment. Others are often unaware they are in a competition with a Three. But this is how a Three experiences inner validation—winning. Threes are often called chameleons because they become whatever it takes to fit and thrive within a milieu. Agile, Threes "can slip into almost any mask and act the part to perfection."[68]

Threes thrive within societies such as capitalism, which also feeds off of competency, comparison and competition. Rohr believes that the Three grows out of affluent cultures: "I am sure that in the Third World countries one would not meet the same percentage of Threes as in the U.S."[69]   Because they are at home and valued in Western culture, they often appear optimistic and cool. According to Palmer, "They do not appear to suffer and may live out

---

65   Riso, *Discovering Your Personality Type*, 67.
66   Rohr, Ebert and Heinegg, *The Enneagram*, 81.
67   Palmer, *The Enneagram*, 135.
68   Rohr, Ebert and Heinegg, *The Enneagram*, 82.
69   Ibid., 89.

their entire life oblivious to the fact that they have lost a vital connection to their own interior life."[70]   If the One values effectiveness, the Three values efficiency; if the One seeks to get things right, the Three seeks to get things done. They seek to achieve in record time in order to move onto the next conquest. This can take the form of degrees, positions, accomplishments and relationships. They also move quickly from thinking to acting. Time is of the essence, and there is much to be done. Often Threes sacrifice deep imagination that comes with reflection and calculation because they move so quickly into action. Comfortable in front of the crowd, personal intimacy and relational connection often lack in Threes because they do not want to risk vulnerability, or come to terms that their inner life is neglected.

Threes are hard to read. Because they place a high value on the exterior life (image, recognition and achievement) they often suppress their interior feelings (anger, rage and embarrassment). Further, they struggle to read others as well. Like Ones, Threes fear failure. However, the Three's fear of failure is rooted in worth and "there is nothing sadder on the Enneagram than an unsuccessful Three."[71] They have a future orientation toward life, which is why they are always aimed out at the next prize. Threes do not shrink back from self-promotion, which partly explains the emergence and flourishing of social media. They are multi-taskers and natural salespeople. Few really ever know Threes because they remain on the surface. The best of Threes are characterized as self-accepting, inner-directed and authentic.[72] The worst of Threes are deeply narcissistic, hurtful to others for personal gain and deceptive.

The lie Threes believe: "It's not ok to have your own feelings."
The truth Threes need: "You are loved for yourself, not for what you do."[73]

---

70   Palmer, *The Enneagram*, 136.
71   Stabile, *Know Your Number.*
72   Riso, *Discovering Your Personality Type*, 69.
73   Stabile, *Know Your Number.*

Type Four

ONE WORD: Individualist

FOUR WORDS: Dramatic, Artistic, Melancholic, Intuitive

SURVIVAL STRATEGY: I must be unique and different.

FAMOUS FOURS: John Keats, Joni Mitchell, Alan Watts, Bette Davis[74]

From Fours, the world receives a great deal of what is good, true and beautiful. Fours are categorized under the feeling triad and are emotional people. These emotions can manifest in ways healthy and unhealthy, hence, the Four is often depicted as a melancholic artist. Preferring individualism, they value authenticity and can easily perceive phony manipulation in others. They seek emotional honesty, inspiration and creating helpful experiences for others. Riso asserts, that healthy Fours want to be true to themselves and they want others to also be true to themselves.[75] This is why it is easy for them to be critical when they perceive falsity in others. Hamlet captures the Four well:

> This above all: to thine own self be true,
> And it must follow, as the night the day,
> Thou canst not then be false to any man.[76]

According to Stabile, there are fewer Fours on earth than any other type.[77] They are complex children who need to feel extra special. Their underlining childhood theme is loss. According to Palmer, "Fours remember abandonment in childhood, and as a result suffer from a sense of deprivation and loss."[78] Fours long for that which they lack; and miss out on what they have.[79] Unconsciously dwelling on what is missing, they lose appeal to what they actually have. Palmer continues to describe scenarios of Fours

74   Palmer, *The Enneagram*, 193.
75   Riso, *Personality Types*, locs 2529-2531.
76   William Shakespeare, *Hamlet: A Tragedy in Five Acts* (New York: S. French, 1800), 78– 80.
77   Stabile, *Know Your Number*.
78   Palmer, *The Enneagram*, 168.
79   Ibid., 169.

accordingly: "If you get the job, you want the man. If you get the man, you want to be alone. If you are alone, you want the job and man again. Attention cycles to the best in what is missing and, by comparison, whatever is available seems dull and valueless."[80]

They are moody and struggle to be satisfied. When it comes to vocation, Fours seldom settle for routine jobs. They would rather be true to their talents and poor than rich "sellouts." Often their main concern is relationships, which trend toward inconsistency at best, and volatile at worst. Romantically, they love the pursuit. Once in a romantic relationship they can feel bored because the quest is over. With friendships they are often the first to stand in solidarity with other people's pain. Fours are excellent at "Sitting Shiva" and are attracted to the Church season of Lent. They are attracted to extremes and can sometimes manufacture drama in order to feel alive.[81]

Their orientation toward life is often romantic, aesthetic and artistic.[82] This does not mean they always have musical instruments, microphones or paint brushes in hand, but they often do. They often express their feelings in dance, music, painting, acting and literature.[83] Fours can unlock beauty in the world for others. When they feel stuck in the real world, Fours "reinforce their sense of self through fantasy and the imagination."[84] Fours interiorize life, which can spawn self-absorption, depression and introversion. They are also prone to critical spirits and pervasive negativity. They must learn to discern the difference between having a critical mind (analyzing life) and cultivating a critical spirit (negative outlook toward others).

Spiritually Fours reject the categories of sacred and secular. They want to see both worlds come together in a coalescence of beauty and harmony. According to Rohr, they prefer symbols and dreams to mechanics and pragmatics.[85] Although they claim to have

---

80   Ibid., 170.
81   Stabile, *Know Your Number.*
82   Riso, *Discovering Your Personality Type*, 69.
83   Rohr, Ebert and Heinegg, *The Enneagram*, 98.
84   Stabile, *Know Your Number.*
85   Rohr, Ebert and Heinegg, *The Enneagram*, 98.

thrown on a few clothes as they rushed out the door, their fashion is carefully selected. They want others to notice them for the way they stand out. Aesthetically attractive, Fours can also appear "esoteric, eccentric, extravagant, or exotic."[86] Possessions bring Fours little joy as they much prefer longing. In the words of Rohr, "longing is more important than having."[87] This is why the pursuit of life is more satisfying than the attainment of it.

The minds of Fours can transfix on an unalterable past mistake. Their inner monologue repeats phrases like, "if only, if only." This inner sense of disappoint yields seasons of self-isolation, particularly socially. The Four may be with you in the room physically, but can mentally, spiritually and emotionally be as far from you as the moon. In a weird psychological twist, Fours can grow to be attracted to pain, loss and seasons of darkness. When a Four feels like a failure, anger swells within. Their thoughts can easily turn morbid and self-hatred becomes their disposition. This leads to feelings of despair, hopelessness and self-destruction. Many who contemplate suicide are Fours because the interior worldview they have constructed is so heavy that they believe this must be all there is, therefore, they wonder, "what is the point of living?" Drugs and alcohol are common release valves for Fours as coping mechanisms of escape.[88]

The lie Fours believe: "It is not ok to be too functional or too happy."
The truth Fours need: "You are seen and valued for who you are."

Type Five

ONE WORD: Investigator

FOUR WORDS: Perceptive, Detached, Informed, Introverted

SURVIVAL STRATEGY: I must be knowledgeable and equipped.

FAMOUS FIVES: Rene Descartes, Emily Dickinson, Meryl Streep, Franz Kafka[89]

---

86 Ibid.
87 Ibid., 99.
88 Riso, *Discovering Your Personality Type*, 70.
89 Palmer, *The Enneagram*, 233.

The investigator's personality is like a castle. Imagine a high, impenetrable structure with tiny windows at the top.[90] This is the Five. The windows at the top are but the tiniest openings where others can peer in. Whereas they have developed a greed for knowledge, they also seek privacy. They learned as children that the world can be dangerous and privacy stolen. Many Fives report others intruding on them at a young age that led them to cultivate an inner world within which only they could access. Many Fives also report feeling little tenderness and intimacy in childhood, which explains why they are characterized as thinkers who are out of touch with emotional resources. [91]

Fives have a tendency toward keeping their lives secret because they struggle to trust others. Many of them are introverted and lead a strategic, compartmentalized life. Because Fives work so hard to acquire the depth of their knowledge base, they often hoard their knowledge from others. For them knowledge equals power, so it is best to not give it all away. Of all the types, Fives are the most emotionally detached. This means they are able to experience a feeling and let it go. Feelings do not imprison them. They can think their way out of most predicaments. [92]

Rohr claims that Fives are prone to a kind of emptiness, which explains why they, unlike Fours, pursue fulfillment.[93] They are always in search of the next book, seminar, silent retreat, advanced degree or self-advancement theory. They tend to enjoy travel, plotting out museums and educational places of interest. Thus, European cities are more interesting destinations than the beaches of the Caribbean. Fives are constantly preparing and equipping themselves. The pursuit of data acquisition is an adequate way to sum up a Five. They feel that acquiring the necessary knowledge and skill in the present will equip them for the task in the future. Fives love developing their minds, and will do so at the expense of engaging their bodies. Because they are mentally alert, little escapes their no-

90   Ibid., 204.
91   Rohr, Ebert and Heinegg, *The Enneagram*, 115.
92   Stabile, *Know Your Number*.
93   Rohr, Ebert and Heinegg, *The Enneagram*, 115.

tice; "They value foresight and prediction."[94]   Fives are devoted to mastering what they deem worthwhile and can concentrate on single projects for great lengths at a time.

One of the greatest gifts of a Five is their emotional neutrality, and they can apply this to others. As objective experiencers of life, they make great judges because they can easily discern fact from empathy. They are thoughtful and careful in all they do. Viewing others as irrational, Fives are independent and rarely react to life. Rather, they prefer to act in their own time and only after they have thought through the best course of action. Fives are the Type who prefer not to argue in real time, but return to the debate days later after they have mentally processed the issue at hand.

They are adept to make good use of time and can finish projects independently and timely. Fives seek to know boundaries, expectations and deadlines in advance. In meetings they prefer written agendas handed out before arrival. They also like to know what time precisely the meeting will end. They enjoy personal freedom, can be dry humored, full of wit and sarcasm. Many experience them as good listeners who like to learn from all they observe. Stabile says, "If you ask them what they 'feel' they'll tell you what they 'think.'"[95]   Further, just as they are secretive they also keep other's secrets, thus making good confessors.

Because Fives are committed intellectuals, they can become argumentative and cynical. Further, they are prone to live in the world of theory and concepts rather than pragmatism and materialism. Riso observes, "They act like 'disembodied minds,' more preoccupied with their visions and interpretations than reality, becoming high-strung and intense."[96]   At their worst, Fives can become reclusive and nihilistic.[97] Many note that schizophrenic tendencies are the pathology of an unhealthy Five. The character portrayed by Russell Crow in the film, "A Beautiful Mind," is a good example of a Five at its worst psychologically.

---

94   Riso, *Discovering Your Personality Type*, 71.
95   Stabile, *Know Your Number.*
96   Riso, *Discovering Your Personality Type*, 71.
97   Ibid.

Many experience Fives as extremely loyal, lifelong friends. In the world of social media, Fives prefer not to self-promote, compete or demonstrate superiority. They will often use social media to stay abreast with other's lives rather than utilize it to display their own. According to Palmer, "Fives can mask feelings of superiority over those who crave recognition or success."[98] Independently wired, they often do not need the approval of others for positive self-esteem.

The lie Fives believe: "You are strong enough to not need the assistance and comfort of others."

The truth Fives need: "Your needs are not a problem."

Type Six

ONE WORD: Questioner

FOUR WORDS: Fearful, Loyal, Procrastination, Committed

SURVIVAL STRATEGY: I must be secure and safe.

FAMOUS SIXES: Woody Allen, Jane Fonda, Sherlock Holmes, Hitler (counter-phobic)[99]

At best Sixes are loyal friends and can act heroically for a cause. They are tremendously gifted and make great contributors on a team. Yet the average Six is suspicious of other's motives, particularly due to childhood memories of being let down by authorities. As a result, Sixes either seek a protector or challenge authority in the role of the "Devil's Advocate."[100] They struggle to trust the authority that others wield. Whereas they find solace in the law, the military, the Church and community, the authority figures in organizations, the Church and superiors are always suspect to them. According to Stabile, "The world is a slippery slope full of agendas." [101]They worry about possible future events. They can even fear their own success because of the possibility of loss. With a tendency to

---

98   Palmer, *The Enneagram*, 205.
99   Ibid., 264.
100 Ibid., 237.
101 Stabile, *Know Your Number.*

overreact when under stress, Sixes often blow circumstances out of proportion and are perceived as edgy, angry and pessimistic.[102]

Their root sin is fear, which explains why they have problems with follow-through. Riddled by a history of starts and stops they have held many jobs, initiated several degree programs and a trail of unfinished projects. Sixes frequently find good excuses why they cannot continue in one trajectory. Once they begin a project, they question it. Procrastination is common in Sixes. They live with self-doubt and, as a result, anxiety to act. They find it easier to question than act. Cognitively driven, Sixes reside in the head triad rather than feeling or gut.

Thinking replaces doing for the Six. According to Palmer, "The antiauthoritarian stance makes Sixes gravitate toward underdog causes."[103] Believing others are manipulative, they rarely receive compliments given. Rooted in fear, they constantly scan their environment for signs of danger, easily perceiving falsity and power plays in others. A Six at worst is paranoid. It takes a long time to develop trust, but they are often committed to long marriages because of their tendency to "take on the problem in the marriage."[104] Unhealthy Sixes easily project their own feelings onto others. If a Six considers an affair, they often assume their partner is too, and can treat them accordingly.[105]

Of all the types, Six is the most complex. There are two kinds of Sixes according to Palmer: phobic and counter-phobic. Whereas some Sixes play into their personality type (phobic), others will fight it (counter-phobic). She writes, "A phobic type will vacillate, replacing action with analysis, filled with contradiction and self-doubt. . . . A counter-phobic will overcompensate fear by becoming the sky-diving champion in order to master his fear of heights."[106] Phobic Sixes are characterized by cowardice. Counter-phobic Sixes take unnecessary risks.[107] This complexity makes Sixes hard to

---

102 Riso, *Understanding the Enneagram*, loc 4898.
103 Palmer, *The Enneagram*, 238.
104 Ibid., 257.
105 Ibid., 260.
106 Ibid., 240.
107 Rohr, Ebert and Heinegg, *The Enneagram*, 137.

spot, particularly because counter-phobic Sixes can be mistaken for Eights. Last, Sixes resist authority. Thus, theories such as the Enneagram make them suspicious and resistant to assessment. One will rarely find a Six in an Enneagram workshop. Sixes need safe places to go. Once they perceive safety they are able to achieve great things and make wonderful allies. According to Rohr, Sixes are the most common personality type in Western society.[108] The most common vocation for the Six is school teacher.

The lie Sixes believe: "It is not ok to trust yourself."
The truth Sixes need: "You are safe."[109]

Type Seven

ONE WORD: Enthusiast

FOUR WORDS: Entertaining, Accomplished, Uninhibited, and Manic

SURVIVAL STRATEGY: I must be fun and entertained.

FAMOUS SEVENS: Henry David Thoreau, Peter Pan, Kurt Vonnegut, Groucho Marx[110]

Sevens exude joy and optimism. They are the men and women at the party who enliven the room. Full of idealism and hope, they give the impression that everything is good and beautiful.[111] They are charming and funny, but often carry a childhood wound deep within them, which they avoid at all costs through the search of new experiences and endless activity. Appearing to be full of heart, Sevens actually operate from the head. Strategically motivated:

> In the course of their development many Sevens have had traumatic experiences, which they did not feel equal to.

---

108 Ibid., 131.
109 Stabile, *Know Your Number.*
110 Palmer, *The Enneagram,* 301.
111 Rohr, Ebert and Heinegg, *The Enneagram,* 146.

In order to avoid the repetition of this pain in the future, they have evolved a double strategy: First they repressed or whitewashed their negative and painful experiences. Many Sevens paint their life story in positive colors, even when the scenario was anything but beautiful. . . . Secondly, they've gone into their heads and begun to plan their lives so that every day will promise as much "fun" and as little pain as possible. . . . Sevens would love to live and die at Disneyland.[112]

Sevens are impulsive, responding quickly to personal impulse and desire. They seek adrenaline rushes through change, stimulation and new experiences. Delayed gratification is the furthest thing from their minds. As a result, Sevens are susceptible to various addictions, including chronic anxiety. Riso believes Sevens will choose quantity over quality almost every time.[113] Further, to Sevens, happiness is something to be attained from the outside rather resourced from within. The next drink, the next party, the next achievement, the next joke, the next relationship is the driving motivator for the Seven. Everything needs to scale into bigger, better and more exciting. Of the fruit of the Spirit listed in Galatians 5:22-23, self-control is the most elusive and joy is ostensibly the most present.

Much of their activity "is a flight from the painful abysses of their own soul."[114] Because they spend much of their time protecting the image that everything is wonderful, they rarely let anyone too close. Relational commitment and vulnerability are often elusive to them. It would be too painful, they think, for someone to know their whole story. Pain is not to be felt but shifted. At funerals they move quickly to tell how blissful it must be for the deceased to finally be in Heaven. Unlike Fours, after the loss of a loved one, "Sitting Shiva" would be the last

---

112 Ibid.
113 Riso, *Understanding the Enneagram*, loc 4927.
114 Rohr, Ebert and Heinegg, *The Enneagram*, 147.

thing a Seven would seek. Sevens, therefore, have no clue how to grieve.[115]   In fact, grieving means one is doing something wrong in life. Rohr believes these kinds of rationalizations demonstrate their reliance upon cognition as their driving impulse. Similar to Threes, they are in constant danger of ego inflation.[116]   Where Threes avoid failure, Sevens avoid pain.

Whereas the Six is pessimistic, the Seven is optimistic. Note though that optimism is often a strategy to avoid reality—which can be painful. Therefore, the Seven aims to avoid emotions when possible. This is why they are more prone to addiction than any other type. Avoidance of pain, discomfort and the ugly is a central value. They are also future-oriented people. The future is always bright, which helps them reframe present struggles. Travel is a value because it can remove present heaviness and does not require relationship in the day-to-day. Experience is another value because it can be employed to overcome emptiness. The problem, however, is that once the experience is over, the emptiness returns. Thus, another experience is then required. This partly explains why Sevens more than any type have suicidal tendencies at worst. Sevens can reframe any negative into a positive—until they cannot. When they hit this wall it can turn abusive toward others and life threatening toward themselves.

Underneath their facade, Sevens are often heavy. They succumb to the pressure to always be the life of the party. Others reinforce this pressure because they seek the Seven to entertain them. Although they make it look effortless, Sevens can experience stress to live up to other's incessant expectations. Rohr claims that where Twos store up love, Sevens store up happiness. The charismatic movement is full of Sevens where it is Easter all year. Stable, secure and predictable is a Sevens worst nightmare. Like Fours, office jobs are difficult for Sevens. However, Sevens can function at an extremely high capacity, are exceptionally talented, and have the ability to focus on one thing for a long

115 Stabile, *Know Your Number.*
116 Rohr, Ebert and Heinegg, *The Enneagram*, 148.

time—that is, until they get bored and need to move on to the next thing.

The lie Sevens believe: "It is not ok to depend on anyone for anything."
The truth Sevens need: "You will be taken care of."[117]

Type Eight

ONE WORD: Challenger

FOUR WORDS: Self-confident, Decisive, Just, Leader

SURVIVAL STRATEGY: I must be strong and in control.

FAMOUS EIGHTS: Martin Luther King Jr., Jesse Jackson, Sean Penn, Friedrich Nietzsche[118]

Early in life Eights came to believe that being soft is a disadvantage. Therefore, they compensate with strength, directness and can be quite confrontational. Sometimes their strength is a survival strategy from childhood in order to not be taken advantage of or to prove oneself fit for a social group (gangs proving their courage to peers). They often take charge of a situation because they fear being under unjust authority. They are ready and willing to fight for the underdog. According to Rohr, outsiders confuse them with Ones because of their aggressive personality. Sex and fighting are both ways for the Eight to connect with others.

Energized by disagreement, Eights see life through a lens of black and white. People are either friends or enemies and situations are either right or wrong. They are intense.[119] They rarely apologize and admit mistakes with difficulty because of the appearance of weakness.[120] Eights mistrust others until proven otherwise, believing the world to be hostile and threatening. Their disposition toward others is an "against" stance. Fortunately, Eights have an acute perception for injustice and, more often than not, are willing to stand against it. They can be great leaders as they intuitively expand themselves to fill whatever need exists

---

117 Stabile, *Know Your Number.*
118 Palmer, *The Enneagram,* 340.
119 Stabile, *Know Your Number.*
120 Rohr, Ebert and Heinegg, *The Enneagram,* 163.

in a given moment. Protecting the cause of the weak, Eights are not afraid to use their strength in just causes.[121]   Thus, Eights make great leaders of movements. Many attorneys are Eights. However, at times the honesty they demand from others is not first applied to themselves.

Whereas Ones reform a system from within, Eights launch attacks against the system until it changes or collapses. They avoid all perceptions of weakness, helplessness and subordination. Contrary to expectation, Eights struggle not as much with rage/anger as they do with passion. They are lusty, desirous people who follow their gut instincts. At worst, this means that they have a tendency exploit others and not respect their dignity. Enjoying retaliation, healthy Eights learn to restrain their strength and channel it into helpful directions. For example, in the civil rights era, Martin Luther King Jr. learned the strength of non-violence rather than brutal force to effect change. Unhealthy Eights are accused of controlling others. However, what they seek is to not be under the control of others. A toxic romantic relationship with an Eight often veers into feeling possessed or dominated.

One of the most interesting facets of Eights is how often they are misinterpreted by others. [122] They are more tender than people perceive. Often their harsh outer shell belies their soft interior. Few people come to recognize this in Eights because they spend energy hiding what is underneath. Among many reasons for this interpretation is the fact that they speak in imperatives, are impatient with indecision, and struggle when others "beat around the bush."   [123]Rarely do Eights notice how others perceive them to be off-putting or aggressive. To them, skirting around the truth is disrespectful. Whereas they seldom bully others, their main competition is themselves.

The lie Eights believe: "It is not ok to trust just anybody."
The truth Eights need: "You will not be betrayed."[124]

---

121 Ibid.
122 Stabile, *Know Your Number.*
123 Ibid.
124 Ibid.

Type Nine

ONE WORD: Peacemaker

FOUR WORDS: Peaceful, Reassuring, Complacent, Neglectful

SURVIVAL STRATEGY: I must maintain peace and calm.

FAMOUS NINES: Julia Child, Eisenhower, Pope John XXIII, Frodo Baggins[125]

Nines often recall childhood memories of feeling over-looked. Over time they began to believe that the interests and needs of others were more important than their own. They are often interpreted as people who are numb to the world. Twos and Nines look alike. They can easily go with the flow, preferring not to set the pace but, rather, to assist others along the way. Nines best exude the proverbial question, "Can't we all just get along?" It is said of Nines that they have difficulty discerning what tasks are urgent from those that are not. Thus, they can find themselves with many to-do items, but unsure which to tackle first.[126] Palmer avers that as they lose contact with their personal longings because of the importance they place into other's desires, they divert energy into inoculating activities such as watching TV. They lack focus and determination.

Fearing separation from others, Nines do not like to say "no" to others. They often do not place greater importance on their opinions, so it is easy for them to be persuaded towards another's point of view simply because they can easily see all view points as valid. A Nine's decision in a conflict can sometimes be no decision. However, they make excellent mediators. Whereas Eights make great attorneys, Nines make great judges because of the ability to be objective. They are able to express harsh truths in a calm manner, which helps others receive their words.[127] According to Palmer, "Their burden is that they suffer from not knowing what they want, and their blessing is that by having lost a personal position, they are often able to intuitively identity with other people's inner experience. If you identity with each of the Ennea-

---

125 Palmer, *The Enneagram*, 345.
126 Ibid.
127 Rohr, Ebert and Heinegg, *The Enneagram*, 178.

gram types, you are very likely a Nine."[128]

Nines like ritual, familiarity and peace. Appearing humble, Nines are usually insecure and belittle themselves.[129] They are known to struggle with laziness. The upside of that vice is that they are prone to non-violence. To their detriment, they leave the most important tasks of the day to complete at the end, replacing essential needs with non-essential substitutes.[130] Due to repressed anger, Nines can suffer from inner turmoil and passive aggression. They are similar to Twos and have difficulty maintaining a personal position. The reason for this is because they are more concerned about whether they agree or disagree with another's viewpoint rather than developing their own. People sometimes misinterpret their silence for tacit agreement even though they may be undecided. Others report Nines to be on automatic in life. Although incredibly talented and resourceful for others, Nines can take on a load without letting anything go. Over time, this builds up and can lead to exhaustion or emotional implosion. The young Frodo Baggins from the tale, *The Lord of the Rings*, is a classic Nine at the beginning. Motivating him to save the world from evil proves to be a difficult feat—which ironically makes him a viable candidate due to his non-interest in ruling the world as victor. Along the journey Frodo moves into an Eight wing and is transformed for the task.

Whereas an Eight needs to be against something, the Nine seeks to avoid conflict altogether. According to Stabile, Nines "have the least energy of all types because they are internally and externally bounded. Believing a personal agenda threatens harmony, they drop their opinion and go along with others."[131] Of all the types, they are the least controlling. They often remain in long relationships; they enjoy nature, are good in ministry positions and savor the simple pleasures in life.

The lie Nines believe: "It is not ok to assert yourself."
The truth Nines need: "Your presence and opinion matters."[132]

---

128 Palmer, *The Enneagram*, 348.
129 Rohr, Ebert and Heinegg, *The Enneagram*, 181.
130 Palmer, *The Enneagram*, 348.
131 Stabile, *Know Your Number*.
132 Ibid.

3

INTRICACIES OF THE TYPES

Triads

The nine personality types are arranged in three "triads."[133] According to Riso and Hudson's work, *The Wisdom of the Enneagram*, "The triads are important transformational work because they specify where our chief imbalance lies. The triads represent the three main clusters of issues and defenses of the ego self, and they reveal the principal ways in which we contract our awareness and limit ourselves."[134] Types Eight, Nine and One are located in the gut triad. This means they are often motivated to act based upon instinct. It does not mean they are disconnected from mental and emotional processes, but that they most rely on instinct to make decision. According to Rohr, "Their center of gravity lies in their underbelly . . . (they are) immediate, spontaneous, felt and intuitive."[135] It is also theorized their primary orientation is "against" others.[136] Types Two, Three and Four are located in the feeling triad. Utilizing emotions as the primary way to guide behavior, the heart is the symbolic organ to refer to these types. There is, however, some debate among Enneagram experts as Suzanne Zuercher "criticizes the heart type because the persons actually have no genuine access to their own feelings. They experience themselves in reaction to the feelings of others. They can't stay by themselves and unceasingly develop activities to secure the devotion and attention of others."[137]

---

133 See Appendix F.
134 Riso and Hudson, *Wisdom of the Enneagram*, 49.
135 Rohr, Ebert and Heinegg, *The Enneagram*, 36.
136 Ibid., 37.
137 Ibid.

Their senses of touch and taste are emphatic. This triad generally moves "toward" others.[138] Types Five, Six and Seven live from the head or mental center. The primary sense they depend on in life is the eye. Due to their cognitive preoccupation, their orientation is "away' from others.[139] Last, it is helpful to note that the medical field divides the parts of the brain into three categories—root brain (instinctual), limbic system (emotional) and cerebral cortex (thinking brain).[140]

In Appendix J, one can locate the image that is most important to triads. The shape within the Enneagram is referred to as the equilateral triangle, and thus the tips of each point distinguish the three primary personalities—nine, three and six. According to Riso and Hudson's research in Personality Types,

> The Three, Six, and Nine—as the "primary" personality types because they have the most trouble and are the most blocked in some way with feeling, thinking, or instinct. The One, Four, Two, Eight, Five, and Seven on the hexagram— are the 'secondary' types because they are more mixed and not as out of touch with feeling, thinking, or instinct.[141]

Types are vital to the transformative application of the Enneagram. Rather than arbitrarily assigning spiritual practices based upon types, the triads provide greater understanding to how the individual processes life experiences. Therefore, with greater accuracy one can engage practices that both coincide with personality and challenge personality. In this way, transformation becomes possible. As an example of this, Richard Rohr suggests there are three primary ways to pray: "From the inside out (heart types) — want to express themselves, From the outside in (head types), From the

---

138 Ibid., 38.
139 Ibid.
140 Riso and Hudson, *The Wisdom of the Enneagram*, 50.
141 Riso and Hudson, *Personality Types*, loc 634-636.

void (gut types)."[142]   Therefore, prayer that comes naturally (later referred to as "downstream practices") for heart types begins with awareness of what someone is feeling. The prayer of Ignatius is a great example of this kind of prayer. Prayer that comes naturally for head types might begin with reading content from Scripture. *Lectio Divina* is a great practice for head types. Prayer that comes naturally for gut types may find stillness as meaningful. Therefore, centering prayer would be transformative. Triads assist the seeker in greater self-understanding for the purpose of engaging specific, transformative practices.

Ultimately, the triads are driven by particular fears attached to the ego. Consider the following examples of how the types in each triad subconsciously manage life through fear that if reality were faced, much of human behavior would be the result of illusion supplied by the ego (or false self):

> The Instinctive Triad (Eight, Nine, and One): If I let my guard down and relax, I will disappear. I cannot protect myself if I am truly open. If I really let the world in . . . I will lose my freedom. I will be annihilated.

> The Feeling Triad (Two, Three and Four): If I stop identifying with this image of myself, my worthlessness will be revealed. Deep down, I suspect that I am a horrible, unlovable person, so only by maintaining this ego project do I have any hope of . . . feeling good about myself.

> The Thinking Triad (Five, Six, and Seven): If I stop figuring out what I need to do, the "ground" will not be there to support me. The world cannot be trusted—without my mental activity I will be left vulnerable. If my mind does not keep "swimming," I will sink.[143]

---

142 Rohr, Ebert and Heinegg, *The Enneagram*, 246.
143 Riso and Hudson, *The Wisdom of the Enneagram*, 370.

Novices to the Enneagram should begin with triads before reading all the various types. The reason for this is to start with the large triadic categories as a launching point into the theory. From there, it is easier to know where to delve specifically into the types once one assesses which center (instinctual, feeling or thinking) primarily drives behavior. Triads are most useful in the beginning stages of Type assessment, and, as Chapter 5 will elucidate, when selecting spiritual practices for life transformation.

Wings

The Enneagram are known as nine faces of the soul. Together, in their healthiest expressions, some believe they are the fullness of God. This means that God's presence is best identified through community rather than individuality. Tangentially, the Enneagram is a case for the beauty and mystery of the Church. For some (particularly Sixes who are suspicious of authority) the Enneagram appears confining and limited. After all, if all humans are only one of the nine Types, why are not all Threes exactly alike, or all Sevens, or all Fives? This is where Wings play a vital role. As Riso and Hudson articulate in *Personality Types*, "Most people are a unique mixture of their basic type and one of the two types adjacent to it on the circumference of the Enneagram. One of the two types adjacent to your basic type is called your 'wing.'"[144] Further, Helen Palmer believes, "No two people who belong to the same type are identical, although they share the same preoccupations and concerns."[145] Precisely due to this reality, it is imperative to treat spiritual formation as a diverse endeavor requiring many applications rather than a monolithic, general pursuit where disparate people are given limited disciplines for formation purposes. Appendix A displays a basic view of the nine Types. Once one secures their Type, the variance of their personality is that they lean toward one direction or another.

---

144 Riso and Hudson, *Personality Types*, loc 860-862.
145 Palmer, *The Enneagram*, 42.

Consider the image below.
Figure 2. Wings

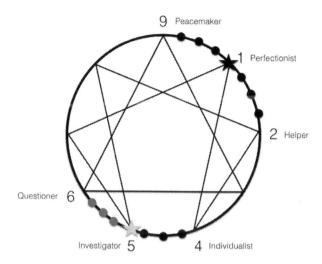

Similar to ticks on a clock, some Types extend further toward their Wing than others. This is one way to account for personality variance within each Type. In the case above, the Type is a Five because of the Wing, which was identified as a Wing Six due proclivity to living with fearful anticipations. This proclivity provided Type assessment

One of the many insights that a wing can offer is assessment of one's primary Type. Some of the Types share much in common. Therefore, it can be difficult to discern between Threes and Eights, Eights and Sixes (counter-phobic), Ones and Fives, and Nines and Twos. The image above demonstrates how one who is split between Types One and Five can secure their core personality through identifying the Wing. Riso and Hudson contend: "Your basic type dominates your overall personality, while the wing complements it and adds important, sometimes contradictory, elements to your total personality. The wing is the 'second side' of your overall personality, and you must take it into consideration to understand yourself or someone else."[146]   Additionally, Riso avers from his work, *Enneagram Transformations*, transformations for the personality type of one's wing. A persom may find that, in certain circumstances, the issues presented by her wing will be more significant than those of her basic type."[147]   In other cases, however, the influence from the Wing will be slight. One's wing, therefore, adds to the uniqueness of personality Type and can assist in type assessment.

One of the frequently asked questions about Wings is whether there is variance from one side of their Type to the other. For example, from the image above, since core personality Type does not change, is it possible to go from Type Five, Wing Six to Type Five, Wing Four? Richard Rohr attempted to answer this question through a lens he named "First and Second halves of life."[148] He suggests that for the first half of life, a person veers toward one Wing; the second towards the other. These halves are not designated chronologically by years, but rather, by maturity. Therefore, one can and often does shift from one wing to the other at some point in life, but without variance in their Type.[149]   Another facet of the Wing to bear in mind is that both Wings can influence the Type. However, one will remain more dominant in one Wing over the other depending on the half of life.[150]   In conclusion to a basic understanding of Wings, here are some general examples of the way Wings affect Type:

Type Nine, Wing Eight: The Comfort Seeker

Type Nine, Wing One: The Dreamer

Type One, Wing Nine: The Idealist

Type One, Wing Two: The Advocate

Type Two, Wing One: The Servant

---

146 Ibid.
147 Riso, *Enneagram Transformations*, 37.
148 See Richard Rohr, *Falling Upward: A Spirituality for the Two Halves of Life* (San Francisco: Jossey Bass, 2013).
149 Richard Rohr, "The Wisdom Way: Scripture, Tradition and Experience" (Albuquerque, lecture, Fuller Theological Seminary, April 25 – May 5 2013).
150 Riso and Hudson, *Personality Types*, loc 869.

Type Two, Wing Three: The Host/Hostess

Type Three, Wing Two: The Star

Type Three, Wing Four: The Professional

Type Four, Wing Three: The Aristocrat

Type Four, Wing Five: The Bohemian

Type Five, Wing Four: The Iconoclast

Type Five, Wing Six: The Problem Solver

Type Six, Wing Five: The Defender

Type Six, Wing Seven: The Buddy

Type Seven, Wing Six: The Entertainer

Type Seven, Wing Eight: The Realist

Type Eight, Wing Seven: The Maverick

Type Eight, Wing Nine: The Bear[151]

Vices and Virtues

Daily life is not experienced in a vacuum. Life is filtered through the veils of personality, and personality is driven by ego. To be clear, the ego is not entirely negative, nor can/should one ever seek to be free of the ego. Rather, the aim is a healthy personality, which begins with self-awareness (which is the gift of the Enneagram), then seeking to routinize spiritual practices for growth. Before committing to specific spiritual practices, it is important to understand certain passions (referred to as "vices") the various Types veer toward. Again, they are not mutually exclusive, as each Type will, to some extent, wrestle with many or all of the vices. The vices are analogous to the deadly sins taught by the Desert Fathers. Inversely, each vice corresponds to a virtue. Succinctly put, the purpose of this section is to give each Type a virtue to aim their character toward. Once one assesses this, the selection of practices can more accurately yield the Type's virtue and conquer the vice. Chapter 5 will outline this lucidly. Consider the following graphs.

---

151 Ibid., loc 876.

Figure 3. Vices

Figure 4. Virtues

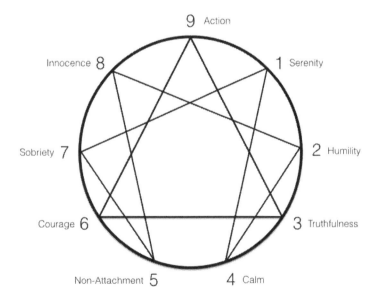

The ego is most susceptible to motivate unhealthy behavior where one perceives personal deficiency. Perception of deficiency, whether illusion or reality drive the various Types to, subconsciously, fill voids within or without. The result of this can be devastating to the person and/or the people around them. Another biblical way of aiming toward a specific virtue that defeats a vice is through an understanding of the fruit of the Spirit from Galatians 5:22-23.

Agriculturally, fruit is derivative from tilling, sowing, watering and exposure to sunlight. Likewise, spiritual fruit is derivative from spiritual practices that permit God's life to sprout from the inside of the person and then out into society. The fruit of the Spirit from the passage above is love, joy, peace, patience, kindness, generosity, faithfulness, gentleness and self-control as an alternative way of viewing the virtues. Fittingly, there are nine fruit of the Spirit. Consider the following graph:

Figure 5. Fruit of the Spirit

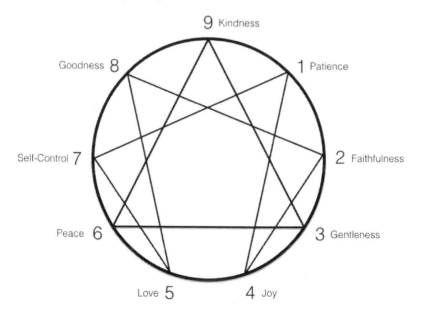

The gift of both the virtues and fruit is orienting toward a character goal. This is in contrast to the vices that surface through perceived deficiency from the ego. As stated previously, none of the fruit listed above are mutually exclusive. Once assessed, spiritual practices can be engaged with increased precision. In conclusion, spiritual formation is a complex, personality specific endeavor. Many communities of faith offer far too few specificities of transformative practices to expect significant life change. On the other hand, it is tempting to choose spiritual disciplines one enjoys without first understanding one's Type well enough to ensure that routine practice with a certain discipline will shape their character. Triads, wings, vices and virtues all provide enhanced self-awareness within each Type to better select practices that transform over time.

PART TWO

Biblical and
Practical Reflection

4

THE BIBLE AND THE ENNEAGRAM

Neglected, dusty and crisp are three characteristics that describe the average Christian's Bible that sits motionless from the bookshelf in many American homes. It often rests just low enough on the shelf to be noticed, yet remains high enough to go untouched. Recent estimates purport 3.9-billion Bibles have been purchased over the past fifty years. Ben Irwin, a creator of the *Community Bible Experience*, rightly suggests a vast difference between "best selling" and "most read." Much has been written on the topic of biblical illiteracy within the twenty-first century, post-Christian society. Pastors are scrambling to motivate their congregations while theologians are bewildered by its neglect. In contrast to many recent voices, perhaps the problem is not that Christians do not know how to read Scripture; it is much more foundational than that. Instead, the vision for why the text matters is often lost.

One of the primary reasons for the decline in biblical literacy is due to the loss of the existential perspective. Christians seldom view themselves through the narratives and teachings of Scripture. Instead, the Bible has been used to report only an historical account of spiritual ancestry. To make matters worse, when the Scriptures are tested through a post-enlightenment analysis of veracity, many conclude them to be unreliable according to modern standards of historical trustworthiness. What this chapter aims to accomplish is narrative identification with each Type, and then a deeper understanding of New Testament texts that the Types can emphasize on the path to transformation. In reclaiming the existential perspective, the reader enters into a dialogue of sorts with the text. In Diane Tolomeo, Pearl Gervais and Remi De Roo's work, *Biblical Characters and the Enneagram*, the authors conclude,

The stories of scripture appeal to our understanding and experience of human beings in diverse emotional states at the same time that they speak to us about ourselves and our inner life. If we see Abraham and Sarah, Moses and Mary, Deborah and Martha, not solely as figures in biblical history but also as representing aspects of ourselves, we begin to understand their stories as intimately connected with our own stories, and they can become mentors in teaching us about our inner lives.[152]

Reading Scripture, then, is an endeavor to close the gap between the saints of old and contemporary lives. Although the twenty-first century is distanced from previous generations due to technological, political and social distinctions, there is much in common one can learn from utilizing the Bible to converse with the past.

The contents of Chapter 4 will pair each Type with a narrative from Scripture and then a teaching from the New Testament. The aim is for the reader to identify with Scripture based on personality. Unlike Chapter 2 where the Types began with One and ascended to Nine, the Types in this chapter will be grouped based upon Triad. Beginning with the instinctive Triad, Type Eight will be first. Moving clockwise, the section will conclude with Type Seven from the Thinking Triad. The reason for this way of grouping is because Types within Triads dynamically relate to one another. As each Type is elucidated, one must bear in mind that the accounts of Scripture are not arbitrary tales, but were recorded for both the purpose of historical veracity, and as a means of personal growth.[153] Tolomeo and cohorts aver, "The diverse biblical characters can be seen to represent aspects of ourselves, both savoury and unsavoury; they are brave and beautiful but also fearful and violent . . . their stories have endured because they are our stories."[154] The goal of this chapter is to accomplish that end, reconnecting the texts of Scripture in a dialogue with contemporary life.

---

152 Tolomeo, de Roo and Gervais, *Biblical Characters and the Enneagram*, 20.
153 Ibid., 21.
154 Ibid. 26.

Type Eight

ONE WORD: Challenger

CORE NARRATIVE: The Syrophoenician (Canaanite Woman)

MEMORY PASSAGE: Proverbs 3:5

Eights are strong people. Decisive, bold and justice centered, Eights are located in the body (feeling) Triad. Often, others
can mistake their power for self-assertion when, in reality, they are
acting on behalf of another. Eights do not necessarily seek to be
in control, but they do seek to avoid being under the control of
another. In the New Testament, both Martha and the Syrophoenician woman exhibit the energy of Type Eight. Neither are afraid to
confront Jesus; they both confront him on behalf of justice done
toward another, and both appear bold and self-confident. This work
will focus the core Eight narrative on the Syrophoenician woman
(Mk 7:24-30). These traits from women, particularly women in
antiquity, strike readers as exceptional and awkward because they
undermine traditional notions of feminine social constructs. Furthermore, Tolomeo wants the learner to reconsider the behavior of
Eights as ungodly: "People who can only imagine a gentle, unchal-
lenging God might want to dismiss the confrontational power of
Eights as lesser channels of the Divine. The Eights, however, bring
to our attention the strong, powerful and just side of the divine presence in our world. In so doing, they become clear manifestations of
Holy Truth."[155] Eights are often the most misunderstood Type.

The Gospel account between Jesus and Syrophoenician
woman is awkward at best. Jesus sought to remain furtive when
arriving in the region of Tyre. Yet the woman, whose daughter had
an unclean spirit, heard he arrived and burst onto the scene to bow
at his feet. This was probably not the incognito evening for which

---

155 Ibid., 154.

Jesus was hoping. As she begged for the release of the demon's stronghold, Jesus awkwardly refused, stating that the children, presumable the descendants of Israel, must be fed before the dogs, implying the Gentiles. To the average reader of the twenty-first century, this image of Jesus messes with traditional conceptions of the Jesus who came to heal, forgive and restore all who asked of him. The woman, a typical Eight, refuses to let injustice win. She fought for her cause and challenged the Son of God that even dogs eat the scraps from the children's table. Meaning there was enough surplus of power for even the Gentiles to get in on the restorative work Jesus arrived to inaugurate. Spellbound by her faith, Jesus pronounces the daughter, who is not present but absent, as healed that very moment. And it was purportedly so.

Evident from the narrative are the following characteristics: the woman's directness, her readiness for debate and an arduous passion for justice.[156] Throughout the narrative the woman is depicted as strong, resolved and willing to confront even a man whose power was greater than her own. She did not appear to want control in the form of receiving a gift to heal the daughter herself. Instead, she wanted to channel the power of Jesus toward the expulsion of demonic activity in her daughter. Eights are typically willing to pay the price for what they deem valuable. In this case, she risked her reputation and social nicety to demand justice for her daughter. The woman is relentless, refusing to take "no" as an answer. Pragmatically wired, she does not attempt to correct Jesus' discrimination (if that is, in fact, what occurred), but employed a strategy to fit within his construct in order to get what she wanted. A brilliant strategy and a classic Eight mentality.

One of the gifts of Type Eight is a big heart. Although misunderstood at times, Eights seek truth above all. One of the distinct differences between an unhealthy and healthy Eight is the basic desire to remain self-reliant.[157] The Syrophoenician woman, in desperation, became healthy when reaching out to Jesus for help.

---

156 Ibid., 164.
157 Riso and Hudson, *Wisdom of the Enneagram*, 74.

This is not an easy thing for Eights to do. Eights should remember that transformation is often most available when metaphorically at a dead end, for it requires the assistance of others. The final aspect to note is the theme of fairness. Both Jesus and the woman argue on the basis of what is fair. After the woman pleads her case of fairness concerning the exorcisms, Jesus is willing to concede and grant her the request. Type Eights are most assertive and dominant when engaging issues pertaining to fairness, justice and truth-seeking. This is the case with the Syrophoenician woman. As Tolomeo incisively writes, "The woman shows the Eight's forthrightness in not being concerned with public opinion when there are urgent things to be done . . . her heart motivates her to become protector of the weak."[158] The core memory verse for Eights is to trust God and not self-reliance. God, in due time feeds the hungry, clothes the sick and provides rest for the broken-hearted. At the same time, God utilizes humans to mediate this love and compassion. Eights must learn to take action, but not outside of God's leading.

Type Nine

ONE WORD: Peacemaker

CORE NARRATIVE: Abraham

MEMORY PASSAGE: Joshua 1:8-9

Nines are the mediators and peacemakers in this world. They reside in the intuitive Triad and often possess a universal benevolence. According to Tolomeo, they are "comforting, unselfish, and accommodating."[159] Due to their ardent desire for peace, they often avoid conflict at all costs, and seek stability in circumstances and relationships. Unhealthy Nines are perceived as slothful and passive, hoping undesirable circumstances will take care of themselves. This is often due to a lack of clear vision, conviction and direction. At their worst, Nines are lazy in their pursuit of trans-

---

158 Tolomeo, de Roo and Gervais, *Biblical Characters and the Enneagram*, 171.
159 Ibid., 244.

formation. The memory verse Nines should commit to memory comes from the book of Joshua (1:7-8): "Be strong and very courageous. Be careful to obey all the law my servant Moses gave you; do not turn from it to the right or to the left, that you may be successful wherever you go. Keep this Book of the Law always on your lips; meditate on it day and night, so that you may be careful to do everything written in it. Then you will be prosperous and successful." Boldness and conviction are imperative for Nines as they embark on the journey of transformation.

Although Abraham sets out on a journey from God of national import, his journey is first one of personal discovery. There are five key moments that occur in Abraham's pilgrimage that identify him as Type Nine. The first scene of his journey is significant. Beginning in Genesis 12, after living seventy-five years in the same location (not surprising for a Nine), Abraham leaves, taking his family on an uncertain journey. His inner monologue is obviously not available, but the text states that Abraham obeyed and left his life of familiarity. The significance of this comes from Genesis 12:1, when God commands him to "go," this word in Hebrew can also be translated, "go to yourself."[160] Although that is not the common interpretation, it is a plausible reading. This first scene demonstrates Abraham's willingness to embark on a journey of transformation within his Type. With slothfulness as the primary vice, an unhealthy Nine would have resisted the call and remained in the land of familiarity.

The second scene in Abraham's narrative, revealing his Type, occurs when they arrive in Egypt to escape famine (Gn 12). The two fear that Pharaoh will kill Abraham if he discovers that Sarah, who is beautiful, is his wife. Determined to mislead Pharaoh that Sarah is his sister, Abraham seeks to avoid conflict at all costs, and even compromises the truth in this instance. Eventually the truth comes out and Pharaoh sends them away with their lives. The third scene occurs in Genesis 15 where Lot and Abraham part ways because of their increasing fruitfulness within geographical

---

160 Robert Alter, *Genesis: Translation and Commentary* (New York: W.W. Norton, 1996), 53.

constraints. Abraham says to Lot, "Let there be no strife between your herders and my herders" (Gn 15:4). He is desirous to maintain peace to the extent of permitting Lot to choose whatever direction he desires. Abraham, then, will go the other way.

Nines will often preserve the peace, even if it means settling for a lesser-than reality. Moreover, they are often out of touch with what they, themselves, want. Still in Genesis 15, the fourth scene occurs. Abraham and Sarah are still barren, having yet to receive God's promise to establish a lineage. Sarah hashes out a plan to have Hagar, the house maiden, birth a child for Abraham in order to continue his line. Soon after she becomes jealous of Hagar and instructs Abraham to cast her out. As in times past, Abraham listens to her and goes along with the plan according to her desires. Once again, Abraham suppresses morality to keep the peace.

By Genesis 17, nearly a quarter-of-a-century has passed and Abraham still has no lineage with Sarah as matriarch. Whereas patience is not a significant challenge to a Nine, the juxtaposition of Abraham's personality from Sarah's is stark. The fourth scene displaying his Type Nine identification can be read in Genesis 18. Learning that God plans to annihilate Sodom for her godlessness, Abraham pleads on behalf of Lot's territory for its preservation. Like many Nines, he assumes a mediation role, attempting to forge peace between God and the many civilians who will imminently lose their lives.

The fifth and final scene to link Abraham with Type Nine is one of the most bizarre and mysterious chapters in all of Scripture (Genesis 22). Abraham is instructed to sacrifice Isaac, his own son and the only child of Sarah. In Jewish oral tradition some circulate that Abraham was a maker of idols in his days of youth. Thus, this was his final test of whether he trusted the Living God, or sought to fashion God into his own desires. Passing the test, Abraham moves to sacrifice Isaac, and just before he plunges the knife, God steps in and supplies a ram instead. Debates have raged for years as to why a good, loving, all-knowing God would require such a vile thing. Just as Abraham's journey as a Type Nine began with self-discovery, so his journey ends with his full transformation. Without a doubt, Abraham learns to trust the voice of God, and act when called upon. By the end of his life, Abraham is fully aware of who he is: "Abraham and Sarah's journey is our own, giving up the familiar lands we know and moving to a place of trusting and connecting with our true selves and with God."[161]

Type One

ONE WORD: Perfectionist

CORE NARRATIVE: The Apostle Paul (Acts 8-28 and Epistles)

MEMORY PASSAGE: Matthew 19:26

Type One belongs to the instinctive (body/gut) Triad. Ones tend to emphasize idealistic and perfectionistic tendencies and are their own worst critic. The biblical narrative Ones may most identify with is the Apostle Paul. Consider the way he defends his credibility to the Philippian Christians. Apparently, legalism had crept back into the community from false teachers. Paul details his resume: "If anyone else has reason to be confident in the flesh, I have more: circumcised on the eighth day, a member of the people of Israel, of the tribe of Benjamin, a Hebrew born of Hebrews; as to the law, a Pharisee; as to zeal, a persecutor of the church; as to righteousness under the law, blameless" (Phil 3:5-6 NRSV). Paul had skillfully and meticulously perfected his resume before encountering a theophany on the road to Damascus.

Sometimes the greatest blessing for Ones is to be "knocked off their horse." The next line of the letter to the Philippians Paul writes that he considered all of his former accomplishment nothing compared to what he received in Christ through faith. At first glance, one may conclude Paul was a healthy Three in this passage. Although there are achiever tendencies in Paul's past, he relates to the One because of his propensity to anger as a vice. Another reason to place Paul into the One Type is because of the quality within

161 Tolomeo, de Roo and Gervais, *Biblical Characters and the Enneagram*, 253.

his achievements. For example, "as to righteousness under the law, blameless." For a Three, the achievement of a Pharisee would be sufficient. But for a One, perfection within that achievement is paramount. Threes are efficient so the title Pharisee is enough. Ones are perfectionistic, so being the best Pharisee of all matters most.

Recall that Ones are also known as reformers. Paul, formerly, Saul, literally killed Jews who followed Jesus. Formerly Saul, an ancient-time religious bounty hunter, when converted received the name Paul, meaning "little one." Ones want to believe they are always right. For Saul to receive the name Paul was nothing short of a transformed encounter within his personality. He had spent his entire life perfecting his resume. In an instant it became rubbish to him as he began a new vocation of transforming his anger into love. This is the reason he emphasizes *metanoia* throughout his works. Imagine a One who has journeyed so far down one path to have to turn around and head the opposite direction. This takes maturity; this is repentance. Unhealthy Ones would often rather be wrong and committed to one path, then right and have to turn around. When Ones realize the error of their ways it can paralyze them in self-pity and deep regret.[162]   Healthy Ones can detach themselves from anger and perfection, admit their flaws and seek restoration. This is Paul's narrative in a nutshell. Moreover, healthy Ones can even utilize their errors of the past to assist others in avoiding pitfalls, which is Paul's writing tactic in Philippians 3.

According to Tolomeo, "The more Paul 'gains Christ,' the more his ego is liberated (Philippians 3:8-9)."[163]   There are other Scriptures that provide Type insight into Paul. After his conversion, he still tends toward self-righteousness and inflexibility at times. This explains some of the conversational tone in his letters, particularly when he confronts Peter and on another occasion parts ways with Barnabus, his former ministry mentor and companion, over a ministerial difference that was non-doctrinal (Acts 15). In the letter to Galatia he wishes that those who unsettle Christians back into le-

---

162 Ibid., 71.
163 Ibid., 74.

galism "should castrate themselves" (Gal 5:12). Inflexibility in Ones toward others can cause great relational rupture. Yet it is the self-rigidity, and self-perfection that can be most crushing when headed in an unhealthy direction within personality. Paul writes to the community in Rome of his inner conflict, "For I do not do the good I want, but I do the very thing I hate . . . for I know that nothing good dwells within (my flesh)" (Rom 7:18-19). An unhealthy Paul would tend toward self-hate and chronic shame. However, healthy Ones are able to repent of sin (and imperfection of every kind), offer their shortcomings to God, and receive restoration through divine grace.

The New Testament Scripture on which Ones should focus, ironically, comes from the Sermon on the Mount: "Be perfect, therefore, as your heavenly Father is perfect" (Mt 5:48). The ostensible curse of this text is the attempt to live up to a standard impossible through the flesh. This is what Paul condemns time and again after conversion. However, Jesus' teaching reminds the reader that perfection is a noble, God-ordained pursuit. Like Paul, it is attainable through repentance and grace. Without cooperation with the Spirit of God, it is impossible. As Matthew would later record, Jesus taught "with mortals it is impossible, but for God all things are possible" (19:26). Therefore, for the One, repentance is the supreme gift of God. Repentance is a cause for joy, not despair. Ones would do well to focus on repentance as a way toward being perfected in this life.

Type Two

ONE WORD: Helper

CORE NARRATIVE: The parable of the sheep and goats (Mt 25:31-46)

MEMORY PASSAGE: Matthew 7:11

Twos belong to the feeling Triad. This Type longs to be loved, which, for an unhealthy Two, is what motivates them to offer love in the form of service to others. Reciprocity is often a value of the Two, so if they give love, they expect a form of love to return to them.[164]   One can see, then, why pride is a challenging vice for this Type. Twos face four preeminent issues: seeking unconditional love, fearing interpersonal rejection, searching for intimacy and needing to nurture others to feel valuable.[165]   Rather than offer a scriptural narrative from Biblical history, a parable will be suggested. Although parables are not historical accounts, they are equally true for they aid in identifying the reader within the text, and imply a pathway toward transformation and wholeness.

The biblical account to best characterize the Two is the parable of the sheep and goats (Mt 25:31-46). The parable is eschatological. Christ returns and begins to parse the nations. Jesus likens one group to sheep and the other to goats. When all is complete the ones at his right hand are invited to partake in the fullness of the eternal Kingdom; the ones on the left are commanded to depart from his presence and enter eternal punishment. This is one of the strongest, most direct parables that Jesus teaches. The difference between the sheep and goats is acts of service. The sheep on the right are praised for the way they cared for poor, oppressed and downtrodden. During their lives, they fed the hungry, gave drink to the thirsty, clothed the naked, visited the sick and those in prison (verses 35-36). The astounding revelation of the parable is how closely Jesus identifies with the poor, the oppressed and the downtrodden. In fact, he sees himself as these people, and when these people are taken care of, Jesus purports that he, himself, is cared for. The implication of the text is that Jesus so cares for the poor that a deed done to them is the same as a deed done to him. Within the greater Roman world, this kind of identification would have been rare at best and most likely unheard of.

Conversely, those parsed to the left are likened to goats who neglected the poor, the broken and downtrodden. They claim to have not seen Jesus as sick, poor or hungry, so they wonder how they could possibly have neglected him, a fair defense for those who do not know just how deeply Jesus identifies with creation. Accord-

---

164 Ibid., 82.
165 Ibid., 95.

ing to Tolomeo, the group on his right "simply did what needed to be done, with no awareness of being unusually good or giving, or the reward of going home with the glow of having done an act of charity. It was just something that happened: done and forgotten." [166]Neither those to his left or his right understood how closely Jesus identifies with the poor.

Nevertheless, it is revealed that Jesus rewards those who love the person in front of them who is in need. And further, to love that person is to love Christ, himself. The lesson through this parable is paramount to the Two because of the "quality of unattachment."[167] The sheep are not even aware of their action. They performed the action and had no expectation in return. This kind of love represents what Durham scholar, John Barclay calls "incongruous grace."[168]

Twos want to be loved, which is the motivating factor for giving love. Jesus is pleased with those who give love, expecting nothing in return. Scripture invites Christians to love because they have already been loved beyond measure. In John's first epistle they love because he first loved (1 Jn 4:19). Healthy Twos recognize the presence of grace and love in the first place. For the Christian, the task for the Two is to solidify her identity in Christ by grace, and then recall her identity through spiritual practices before moving into the tasks of the day. These practices will aid Twos in demonstrating love as an extension of God's love into the world, rather than expecting reciprocity when performing an act of service. The following chapter will detail specifics with regard to helpful practices for this Type. When Twos perform an act of service, they pause and reflect before helping to ensure proper motives. For example, Jesus taught that when giving charity, do not let your left hand know what your right hand is doing (Mt 6:3). Well aware of the human propensity to manipulate and self-deceive, Jesus instructs his followers to practice righteousness in secret so that their motives remain pure and solely unto God.

The core passage Twos should know as they move toward

---

166 Ibid., 83.
167 Ibid.
168 John Barclay, *Paul and the Gift* (Grand Rapids, MI: William B. Eerdmans, 2015).

health is Matthew 7:11: "If you then, who are evil, know how to give good gifts to your children, how much more will your Father in heaven give good things to those who ask him!" Where this passage best connects and instructs Twos is the fact that God, the Father, is both aware of and satisfies one's needs. Once this Type recognizes God's gift and receives it, there is ample resource to be generous and helpful toward others without needing reciprocity to feel whole. God is love, and gives love freely through the gift of the Spirit of Christ, who indwells. To biblically see how this works out in relationship, see the account of Ruth and Boaz from the Hebrew Scriptures. Of all nine Types, Twos most need to apprehend the height, depth and grandeur of the grace God has lavished on those who love him and are called according to this purposes.

Type Three

ONE WORD: Achiever

CORE NARRATIVE: King Saul

MEMORY PASSAGE: 1 Corinthians 13:1

Threes live from the feeling Triad. This does not always mean Type Threes are connected to their own feelings and live from a place of emotional integrity. Rather, unhealthy Threes live from the feelings of controlling other's perception of them. Image is the primary vice for a Three. They, therefore, have difficulty accessing their own feelings. Because success (or the perception of success) is of utmost importance to Threes, mature inner qualities and self-awareness can remain elusive. Often their relationships give the appearance of genuine, yet can remain entirely superficial without their knowledge of it. Tolomeo remarks that unlike Ones, who seek to be perfect, Threes desire to appear perfect in their many endeavors. Ambition, ability to motivate and the craving for success drive Threes in decision-making.[169] For these reasons, the rise and downfall of King Saul is a helpful narrative for this Type.

---

169 Tolomeo, de Roo and Gervais, *Biblical Characters and the Enneagram*, 173.

King Saul and King David were both Threes. This work will focus on Saul. From the onset, neither of the two was born into royalty, but both were raised in rural obscurity. Saul was anointed as the first King of Israel. Before his time, the nation was ruled through a series of judges. The people cried out to God to be like other nations, desiring a King to rule over them. God gave them what they asked in the form of Saul. From 1 Samuel 8, the text is clear that Saul was good looking. This is often extremely important to a Three. First Samuel 9:1 reads, "There was not a man among the people of Israel more handsome than he; he stood head and shoulders above everyone else." Society looks to leadership who embody both competency and the physical appearance of success. Many people debate that in the contemporary world of visual media, a presidential incumbent who is paralyzed or over-weight would, with great difficulty, be elected in America.

When reading 1 Samuel 8-12 one is struck by the good nature of Saul. He does not appear to clamor for image and success. In fact, Samuel finds him and anoints him king rather than Saul demanding pre-eminence. In his early life, Saul appears to be in touch with his feeling center. In fact, when searching for missing donkeys (1 Sm 9:5) he returns home because he senses his father may grieve his absence and begin to worry. This serves as a cue that Saul is self-aware of how others may feel. Some Enneagram experts surmise that Threes often aim to make the family proud from a young age. When Samuel approaches Saul about the prospect of becoming king, Saul is genuinely surprised. His humility is obvious from 1 Samuel 9:21. One of the turning points in Saul's life occurred when he was filled with the spirit of God, and turned into a different person (1 Sm 10:6). Whereas this is a transformative act of God, growing Saul into a powerful king, it later works against him as ambition, entitlement and misusing what he has been entrusted with causes him to seize more power and become jealous. He begins to identify more with the person he becomes than the humble heritage from which he came. It is important for Threes to remain grounded with their past and real relationships in the present that speak truthfully. Otherwise, self-preoccupation can take a Three down, and eventually down Saul went.

There is a definitive turning point of Saul's character two years into his reign. This occurred simultaneously, and relatedly to Samuel transitioning out of his prophetic role alongside Saul. Accountable relationships are vital for a Three. Once Samuel steps out, everything changes (1 Sm 13). Due to Saul's early military success and absence of accountability, he learns to rely on his achievements rather than God's word. First Samuel 13 records an account that displays Saul's commitment to success over obedience. The Philistines are mounting an attack against Israel and Samuel is delayed. Therefore, Saul takes the priestly matters into his own hand and offers the sacrifice before the war. The account is thus:

> (Saul) waited for seven days, the time appointed by Samuel; but Samuel did not come to Gilgal, and the people began to slip away from Saul. So Saul said, "Bring the burnt-offering here to me, and the offerings of well-being." And he offered the burnt-offering. As soon as he had finished offering the burnt-offering, Samuel arrived; and Saul went out to meet him and salute him. Samuel said, "What have you done?" Saul replied, "When I saw that the people were slipping away from me, and that you did not come within the days appointed, and that the Philistines were mustering at Michmash, I said, 'Now the Philistines will come down upon me at Gilgal, and I have not entreated the favour of the Lord'; so I forced myself, and offered the burnt-offering." Samuel said to Saul, "You have done foolishly; you have not kept the commandment of the Lord your God, which he commanded you. The Lord would have established your kingdom over Israel forever, but now your kingdom will not continue; the Lord has sought out a man after his own heart; and the Lord has appointed him to be ruler over his people, because you have not kept what the Lord commanded you."

71

Threes are so determined to succeed, that they take matters into their own hands, often making the original dilemma worse. Efficiency is a significant vice for the Three, and can lead to impatience and self-assertion. For this reason, unhealthy Threes are frustrated in a team dynamic. For Saul matters only down-spiraled from this point. Rather than seeking humility, accountability and repentance, Saul's heart hardens into modes of self-protection, fear and jealousy. This is most evident when young David, a shepherd in rural obscurity slays the giant Philistine that Saul could not. His jealousy would later grow to rage as the people of Israel honored David more than Saul. It would end with Saul chasing David down to end his life. David is the counter-part of Saul. Both Threes, David learns to face his downfalls (sinning with Bathsheba and sending Uriah into impending death) and repent. Saul, on the other hand, never matures as one cover-up leads perpetually to another, resulting in a man who will always be remembered as the treacherous first king of Israel.

The Scripture Threes should commit to mind and heart is 1 Corinthians 13:1. It does not matter what one achieves or fails in. What matters is whether or not the motive behind behavior is love or self-exaltation. Love leads one to greater measures of humility, grace and compassion. Self-exaltation is a downward spiral leading to coercion, jealousy and pride. No matter how ostensibly generous or gifted one may appear, when ambition and achievement is the primary goal, love is never present. For the Church, that is unacceptable in the eyes of God.

Type Four
ONE WORD: Individualist

CORE NARRATIVE: Job

MEMORY PASSAGE: Deuteronomy 6:4

Fours reside in the feeling Triad. They retreat within themselves and are known for their radical commitment to individualism. This often leads to them feeling a certain uniqueness about themselves that separates them from the rest of the world. The Enneagram expert, A.H. Almas, asserts, "Uniqueness is not specialness; all unique beings are expressions of the same divine Source."[170] The "Shema" (Dt 6:4) from the Hebrew Bible is very important for the Four to grasp as he moves toward maturity. Central to faith for the Judea-Christian adherent is to love God and others. Further, it is to recognize that God is One. For one to be in God is not only to recognize his uniqueness—which Ones do so well—but to also notice how he is interconnected just as God is in Trinity. As Riso and Hudson suggest in their work, *The Wisdom of the Enneagram*, the more self-focused and less connected with others one becomes, the more ardently his personality Type can attach to ego as identity.[171] Connectedness is often a missing element in the Four's life that leads to immaturity and, at worst, suicide. For this reason, the biblical narrative to which Fours should pay attention is the rise, fall and triumph of Job.

Job's narrative is about spiritual maturity from an individualist mindset to a cosmic hope. Preoccupied by what he had and then lost, Job is driven to the precipice of despair. Essentially, what this narrative illustrates is how to view God (and humanity) when life does not go as planned. It is a narrative of self-understanding. The reader should not become overly pre-occupied as to whether this account happened, but perceive how this account happens. Theodicy is one of the greatest challenges to speak hope into within a world riddled with terrorism, decay and terminal illness such as cancer. It must be asked, what do the presence of these enemies mean about the nature of God?

Job is a Four in the sense that the author reveals a significant amount of time spent on analyzing feelings. Job's small world has collapsed and disappeared in a matter of days. Although the loss of children, material goods and one's own health is indeed tragic, the reader is left internalizing questions about what all this means, can God be praised in despair, and whether anyone is entitled to what

170   A.H. Almas, *Facets of Unity: The Enneagram of Holy Ideas* (Berkley, CA: Diamond Book, 1998), 197.
171   Riso and Hudson, *The Wisdom of the Enneagram*, 191.

Americans have called "the good life." Further, the reader must answer for himself whether life is entitled or gifted. According to Tolomeo,

> What (Job) has to learn is that speaking tragically or dramatically is part of a self-image that needs to be destroyed. It comes from a belief that things should be a certain way, namely, the way we want them to be. When things do not cooperate with what we want, we take it personally and feel that the universe is against us . . . after all has been suffered, can we accept the innate being of things as they are and not expect or receive any tangible reward, and even leave ourselves relaxed and open to the experience of pain and sorrow?[172]

The transformative issue for Job is not grieving what has been lost. Rather, it is identifying so deeply with what was previously meant to be enjoyed rather than received as identity. Ash Wednesday speaks precisely into this narrative because it reminds disciples that they come from dust and to dust they shall return. Nothing is permanent. All will die. Possessions do not last. Unhealthy Fours take this to mean that life is wholly tragic and, therefore, not worth living. Healthy Fours can recognize this transient reality, and enjoy life as a gift while it lasts. Fours have a transformative decision to make: is life tragic, comic, or is life simply what it is in every season?

Fours tend to withdraw when life takes a circumstantial downturn. Tolomeo asserts,

> Religious joy arises from knowing there is nothing we can do or know about anything compared to the vastness of God. Our response can be to see life therefore as tragic, or to plunge through its suffering and find equanimity. . . . Job, however, does not regard his life as anything but

172 Tolomeo, de Roo and Gervais, *Biblical Characters and the Enneagram*, 201.

tragic. His resignation is not life-giving but imprisoning for him, focusing on his calamity and loss.[173]

Job's temptation, over and against his wife's advice, is not to curse God, but to curse his own life (Job 3:1).

Ultimately, the hard work for the Four is to remember life is a gift to receive. Conversely, the gift of life is fleeting and one cannot cling to what one has as an identity. Transformation lies not only in accessing this perspective but inviting others on the journey that will laugh and mourn together depending on the season. Retreating into a lonely state of woe is not the answer that the Four seeks in despair. One must recall that envy is the core vice for the Four. At the beginning of the account Job lived an envious life not only to his friends, but to the Accuser (Satan) as well. Fours struggle to see the envy others have of them and are preoccupied with envying what they, themselves, feel they lack. Implied in Satan's accusations is the question: "Why him (Job)?" Perhaps even the friend's reflections on Job's great wealth were, "Why not me?" But rarely does one self-reflect when things are good, thinking, "Why me?" or when things are bad, "Why not me?" This reveals one's expectations and entitlements toward life rather than receiving all things as gifts, and being willing to let them go since they are inferior to identity. The narrative of Job is about moving beyond individual pleasure, rewards and blessing and into experiencing a cosmic Deity who is the center of creation. When one begins to do this, lament can take an appropriate place in loss rather than disrupting core identity. This is precisely what occurs when God answers Job with a series of rhetorical questions.

---

173 Ibid., 205.

Type Five

ONE WORD: Investigator

CORE NARRATIVE: Nicodemus

MEMORY PASSAGE: Hebrews 11:32-40

Fives are located in the thinking Triad. They are research-
ers, observers and investigators. They seek to know everything concerning what they are immersed in, and can devote themselves to
one single task at a time. Albert Einstein, who is believed to be a
Five, once wrote that the sole thing he wanted to know was the mind
of God: all the rest was just details.[174] Unhealthy Fives fear incom-
petence and often possess a greed for knowledge that they hoard
for themselves. As a result, Fives may find themselves withdrawn,
isolated and lonely. Since what they know in their heads often remains detached from emotions (heart) and their will (hands), they
seek independence from anything that would make demands from
them. This manifests in running from relationships where their autonomy could be threatened to an unwillingness to use their gifts in
community. Their quest for autonomy spawns disconnection from
others. Healthy Fives have learned the imperative of interconnected
living, and often bless others because of their wealth of knowledge
and insight. Nicodemus, from John's Gospel, was a Five who wres-
tled with truth and the implications of Jesus' teachings if integrated
into the whole of his life. The reader can view his growth in spiritual maturity as the Gospel unfolds. As the Scriptures reveal, in
conversion to the way of Jesus, he loses his status as a Pharisee and
joins a new community of disciples because of the integration of
his convictions into his everyday life.[175]

The process of Nicodemus' conversion narrative—via
investigation—is notable in chapters three, seven and nineteen of
John's Gospel. It is a process which begins "in the dark" (Jn 3:2)
as he furtively seeks Jesus, "the Light" (Jn 1:4), to inquire about his

---

174 Ibid., 220.
175 Ibid., 223.

Messiahship. Nicodemus is a seminal example of Type Five moving from unhealth to health. He is transformed, literally, by the renewing of his mind (Rom 12:1). However, Nicodemus has to learn on his journey that to be fully transformed, he must not only engage his mind, but his heart, and finally his body into willful action. The Engle Scale provides a helpful perspective of the stages Type Five undergoes to arrive at bearing witness to Christ in the public square. [176]Additionally, the contemplative categories of transformation as illumination, purgation and union also describe the process of Nicodemus' conversion.[177] Fives must be permitted three essential ingredients for transformation to occur: information, time and safety. Jesus provides each of these for Nicodemus.

The first time the reader encounters Nicodemus is in John 3. He is a Pharisee, which means his learning in Torah is advanced. He is also curious about Jesus. So curious, John writes, that he comes to Jesus in the night, implying he came in secret. Unhealthy Fives avoid risk at all costs. They keep information stored in their minds and refuse to release it until all mysteries and questions are solved. Nicodemus needs more information from Jesus before following him. When Jesus calls the initial twelve disciples, he does not give them a treatise about his authenticity, nor does he set up a question and answer session to alleviate their fears. Instead, he works a few wonders to support his legitimacy and then invites them to follow him. This strategy does not work with Fives, and it certainly did not work with Nicodemus. The invitation of Jesus into discipleship involves one's body and not mere cognitive assent. Fives are often out of touch with their bodies and prefer to remain in their heads. Nicodemus does not leave his time with Jesus converted. Fives seek rational, reasonable and systematic categories of truth. Jesus often taught in parables, metaphors and paradoxes. To Jesus' teachings that evening, John wrote that Nicodemus' reply was, "How can these things be?" (Jn 3:9). This does not necessarily imply he was cynical. Rather, it means he needed time to process before committing.

---

176 See Appendix K.
177 Tolomeo, de Roo and Gervais, *Biblical Characters and the Enneagram*, 135.

Readers experience Nicodemus again in John 7. Time has passed and chief priests and Pharisees are debating as to why Jesus has yet to be arrested. Nicodemus takes a risk to vocalize his thoughts: "Our law does not judge people without first giving them a hearing to find out what they are doing, does it?" (Jn 7:51). The reader can observe him moving from a withdrawn, inquisitive seeker, to one who is willing to thoughtfully counter the powers in the room. When Fives hold core convictions, they are some of the most compelling and powerful people in the world because they can support their case through careful reasoning and argumentation. Thus, Fives often make great lawyers, professors and writers.

The last place in John's Gospel where the reader encounters the narrative of Nicodemus is chapter 17. Jesus has been crucified and Nicodemus joins Joseph of Arimathea to take care of his body (Jn 19:38-40). According to Tolomeo, "We can infer . . . that Nicodemus had not agreed to the council's decision to arrest and kill Jesus . . . he could no longer observe . . . but would now be one who was himself watched."[178] The man who came to Jesus in the dark was willing to walk in the light of his new convictions that Jesus was the Messiah. This was nothing less than a startling transformation as evidenced by his actions. When Fives act it means they are resolved and convicted. This was no mere gesture of kindness, but a pledge of faith for Nicodemus—a strange pledge as that given the Messiah was now dead. For Fives who seek to better understand their story alongside the biblical narrative, John 3, 7 and 19 provide incisive insight into their Type. The Scripture that Fives should commit to memory is Hebrews 11:32-40. In this passage one must grapple with what it may bodily cost to cognitively hold Christian convictions in a secular world. Truly, the way of Jesus eventually requires a disciple to engage their bodies in what their minds hold to be true.

---

178 Tolomeo, de Roo and Gervais, *Biblical Characters and the Enneagram*, 241.

Type Six

ONE WORD: Questioner

CORE NARRATIVE: Peter walking on water

MEMORY PASSAGE: 1 Peter 5:7

The lion from the Wizard of Oz most assuredly was a Six on a quest for courage. From the Bible, Peter best exemplifies the life of a Six. Sixes often make great leaders. Although their chief vice is fear, healthy Sixes transform fear into courage, and often accomplish great things with those around them. Sixes reside in the thinking Triad. However, due to fear and insecurity, they often distrust their own thoughts and, thus, seek rules and structures for guidance.[179] Whereas this can make Sixes principled, the unintended consequence is a distrust of their own reasoning in decision-making. According to Tolomeo, "Their vivid imaginations can often cause them to get caught up in potential harm or threat in a situation."[180]

No matter how one reads Jesus' famous keys to the Church passage, it is generally agreed that Peter was the leader of the disciples as the eldest, and held that role to one degree or another throughout the remainder of his life. There are many examples in Peter's life that help the reader assess his Enneagram Type as a Six. When faced with a difficult decision in a given situation, Sixes often will distract themselves with a matter less complicated to avoid the issue. Assessing Peter as a Six aids the reader in understanding why he would return to fishing after the crucifixion. Post-crucifixion and pre-resurrection, Peter is fishing because it was a task of familiarity and security within the (then) present quagmire of confusion, betrayal and loss. In Jesus, Peter "had finally found an authority he could trust . . . and with whom he felt safe and secure."[181] Yet even before the crucifixion Peter's fear is seen as crippling. Once Jesus is taken into custody Peter's security deconstructed. Thinking he

---

179 Kathleen V. Hurley and Theodorre Donson, *Discover Your Soul Potential: Using the Enneagram to Awaken Spiritual Vitality* (Lakewood, CO: WindWalker Press, 2000), 75.
180 Tolomeo, de Roo and Gervais, *Biblical Characters and the Enneagram*, 96.
181 Ibid., 99.

might himself be harmed, he fled the scene and permitted his fears to take over, which led to his three denials. The rooster crowing after the third, then, serves as Peter's wake up call.

In fear, Sixes seek to avoid. The oddity of the Six is they seek authority while distrusting authority. After the crucifixion, Peter was dumbstruck because the trust he placed in Jesus ostensibly failed him. Tolomeo provides keen insight into this dynamic:

> The work of transformation for the Sixes consists of taking back the unquestioning allegiance they have given to an outside authority and putting it back into themselves. Jesus' encounter with Peter after the resurrection does this for Peter. By questioning Peter about his love, Jesus helps Peter to look within himself and discover the love within him that is not offered solely in reaction to what is expected of him. Sixes who turn to their inner strength learn to act out of compliance to what they know from within rather than what they have been told by an external authority. . . . After the encounter with Jesus, Peter is able to continue his discipleship out of his newly-found courage and love, even to the point of ultimately suffering martyrdom.[182]

To be clear, this work is not suggesting unhealthy Sixes should look within in the same way a new-age philosophy would prescribe. Rather, the Christian journey toward courage is to cultivate hearing God's voice within, and to act boldly out of what one hears. This is where the deep work of prayer is imperative for the Six. The gift of Peter's narrative from the Bible is that readers encounter a young, recklessly naïve follower of Jesus who matures over the course of decades into a healthy, transformed man of courage.

One of the most famous accounts of Peter's life is when he comes to Jesus on the water. Recorded in Matthew 14:22-33, this

---

182 Ibid., 96.

scene depicts Peter as the counter-phobic Six who naively jettisons the safety of the boat and walks on water toward Jesus. What is incredible about the account is that his walking on water was Peter's own idea. None of the other disciples thought of going out to Jesus, not even the disciple "whom Jesus loved." However, in getting out of the boat Peter first seeks authority to do so: "Lord if it is you, command me to come to you on the water. He said, 'Come'" (Mt 14:28). Yet as often happens with Sixes, as the waves grew in size fear mounted, causing Peter to shrink down from his original inspiration. External circumstances can be paralyzing for Sixes. What began with fixating on Christ devolved into focusing on externals, and Peter sinks. In the moment of sinking Peter cries out to be saved and Jesus "immediately reached out his hand and caught him" (Mt 14:31). Against self-reliance and pop spirituality, the takeaway for the Christian is not to trust oneself. Rather, it is to trust the activity of God's presence within.

Peter is saved not by recovering positive thoughts or optimistic outcomes, but by crying out for Jesus to save; for God to take action. The Christian's dependence is still upon Christ, but in such a way that one must participate and act with God, rather than passively waiting. If Peter had not cried out, perhaps he would have continued to sink to the bottom of the sea in self-reliance. When one looks at the span of Peter's life in the Scriptures, what is evident is that the Peter who learned to trust in God who had come in flesh, would later have to trust in God who would send the Spirit. The task for the Six today is to cultivate awareness for the voice of God who leads and guides in the midst of chaotic circumstances. One Psalmist reminds readers that God makes known the paths of life (Ps 16:11). In due time God reveals all knowledge in order to walk in the way of mystery. Sadly, many Sixes never mature to this point. Yet those who do mature learn the lifelong task to cast their anxieties/fears on God because God cares (1 Pt 5:7).

Type Seven

ONE WORD: Enthusiast

CORE NARRATIVE: Solomon

MEMORY PASSAGE: Ecclesiastes 3:1

The Enthusiast, Type Seven, is located in the thinking Triad. Although they spend much of their free time in social settings, thriving off other's energy, they often suppress thoughts because of a penchant to avoid pain. As previously stated in Chapter 2, Type Sevens are outwardly happy, but often inwardly sad due to painful past experiences. The biblical character that Type Sevens may most identify with is King Solomon from the Hebrew Bible. According to the Tolomeo, Sevens (are) outwardly perceived as busy as a way to avoid "any direct confrontation with their inner wounds." [183] They also seek to have some level of mastery over the thing(s) they ardently pursue. Recalling that Sevens reside in the thinking Triad is insightful when deconstructing both the motives and behavior of Solomon. When David passed the baton to Solomon to reign over Israel (1 Kgs 2-3), he did not know what exactly to do next. Therefore, utilizing his thinking center, he reasoned to go to Mt. Gibeon, which was the highest place of all, and offered extravagant sacrifices there to God. One can already see the excessive nature of Solomon that would later become clearer in his life. The intriguing thing to note is that God did not require Solomon to perform this sacrificial act.

The breakthrough for Solomon, however, came not when he was awake, offering sacrifices he thought would be pleasing to God. Instead, it came in the dead of his sleep. When one sleeps, the mental and bodily centers shut down, while the feeling center remains engaged. It is this center that permits one to dream. In Solomon's dream God asks him what he wants. He responds by asking for wisdom to rule the people (1 Kgs 3:5ff). Tolomeo adds, "With his preferred ways of knowing closed off, Solomon is able to quickly access his feelings. His reply to God comes not from the head but

---

from the heart."[184] The significance of this insight is that Sevens, who often suppress feelings, frequently make life decisions without truly being in touch with their deepest desires. It is for that reason that many Sevens wrestle with addiction, anxiety and excessive outward behavior. Wisdom was unlocked when Solomon got out of his thinking center and into the feeling Triad. Healthy Sevens are able to face their pain and seek healing in order to apply what they feel to what they think in any given situation.

An example of Solomon's wisdom through his Type is when he engaged the two women in dispute over who was the actual mother of a child. When Solomon seeks out the matter, he discerns the truth not by appealing to their cognitive reasoning, but to their feelings (1 Kgs 3:16-28). Requesting the child to be halved by a sword in order for both to women to be happy with a portion revealed the true mother. Solomon settled the matter not through debate, but through appealing to feelings. This is a characteristic of a healthy Seven who understands that feelings carry value and should not be neglected, numbed or glossed over through excessive behavior.

Solomon was characteristically a Seven in his preoccupation with planning toward the future. His vision for the Temple was beyond comprehension to his listeners (1 Kgs 9). Even the Queen of Sheba was impressed. Surrounding nations all took notice of Israel's power, wealth and religious supremacy (1 Kgs 10:23). It was his lack of humility and moderation that makes assessing his Type apparent. He imported 12,000 horses from Egypt, built fleets of ships as never before, imported gold, maintained 14,000 chariots, and loved upwards to a 1,000 women—many of them from foreign nations. Indulgence, as is often the case, was Solomon's downfall. Toward the end of Ecclesiastes, he mourns that all of these pursuits pale in meaning when compared to the eternal God. Excessive pursuits always end in inner emptiness.[185] Some speculate that the number of his wives were a strategy to avoid inner emptiness. What is vital for the Seven to pursue health is the willingness to face pain.

---

184 Ibid., 130.
185 Ibid., 134.

For a Seven who avoids pain at all costs, in the end the cost will only increase in weight, resulting in humiliation, despair and for some, suicidal tendencies.

The Scripture memory verse for a Seven comes from Ecclesiastes 3:1. The author reminds the reader that everything in life has an appropriate time. The implication of this is that not every time is appropriate for everything. All things in moderation deserve a rightful place in proper context. Ecclesiastes is proof that Solomon grew in maturity from experience: "He learned that weeping is as necessary as laughing and that his feelings can support and not undermine his work."[186] The reader learns that Solomon rejects avoidance as a life survival strategy. Solomon learns that a life of distraction and excessive behavior is not the path to flourishing. Sevens would do well to heed Solomon's narrative in 1 Kings and to study Ecclesiastes as a glimpse of where an intemperate life leads.

---

186 Ibid., 138.

5

DISCIPLINES BY TYPE

Information is good, and application is better, but transformation is best. Although many churches currently face the difficult landscape of numeric decline, churches that are growing often send their congregations out on Sundays with a sense of inspiration from the preaching, but with little instruction on how to grow the other six days of the week. The Church in the West does not have an inspiration problem, for the most part. With a wide array of churches to choose from in any given context to access to free podcasts from preachers across the world, the average church goer has more resources at her fingertips than ever before in history.

However, few congregants boast of robust invitations in their local church to grow. Spiritual formation often tends toward generalistic and overly simplistic: attend church on Sunday, read the Bible, pray and give to the local church is the extent of many churches' vision for transformation of human souls. Riso suggests that there is no single spiritual practice that is right for all people in all places at all times.[187] Churches need variety because people are diverse. It is no wonder that many congregants are well informed, yet ill transformed. This is among the great crises in Western Christianity. Fuller Seminary professor, Eddie Gibbs, noted:

> In contemporary Western Christianity, we have little understanding of the concept of discipleship. Those who are evangelized are brought to the point of decision, go through membership and then continue as a part of the worshipping congregation. Western churches suffer from

---

187 Riso, *The Wisdom of the Enneagram*, 344.

a chronic problem of undiscipled church members, an environment that serves as the perfect breeding ground for "nominal Christianity."[188]

Spiritual formation is another way to refer to the biblical vocation of discipleship. Discipleship (and formation) occurs whenever one endeavors to follow Jesus. Following Jesus is an active pursuit where transformation becomes possible. This active pursuit is practices that transform the human person.

A spiritual discipline actively (or sometimes passively) initiates relational contact with God. The various disciplines that expose the seeker to the conscious presence of God lead to character transformation, and ultimately joining God in the renewal of creation. The terms discipline(s) and practice(s) are used synonymously in this work. The significance of the Enneagram is self-awareness. David Brooks writes, "How hard it is to know ourselves, and how hard we have to work on the long road to virtue."[189] Once one becomes more aware of what they "don't know they don't know," that person may then choose practices to best form holistic character in pursuit of Christ-likeness. As Riso and Hudson espouse, "The Enneagram is much more than an interesting way to classify people. Combined with practices to cultivate our awareness, it can be a powerful tool for transforming the ego."[190] Maitra agrees, stating:

> The Enneagram is only a map. The Enneagram and the information about the human soul and its evolution that it reveals are not ends in and of themselves. No matter how fascinating it may seem to pick apart and decipher more understanding from the Enneagram, unless this information is secondary to our direct experience and fulfills the function of enhancing our personal unfoldment, it will do us little ultimate good. On its own, the informa-

---

188 Eddie Gibbs, *LeadershipNext* (Downers Grove, IL: Intervarsity Press, 2000), 79.
189 Brooks, *The Road to Character*, 244
190 Riso and Hudson, *Understanding the Enneagram*, locs 4739-4740.

tion contained within the enneagram and within this book is not a panacea—it will not solve our problems, resolve our issues, or connect us with our depths. It is only information, whose function is to orient and guide us in our inner work, and unless that knowledge is put to use, we do not benefit from it. If it only remains intellectual, it may stimulate our minds and provide interesting diversion and entertainment, but this should not be mistaken for the actual work of transformation. That endeavor is neither rapid nor is it easy. [191]

The work of Maitri is useful, among other reasons, for the way she demystifies the Enneagram. The Enneagram yields self-awareness, which imparts information to pursue practices where God can transform human character. In his work on Franciscan spirituality, Rohr writes, "We all—by necessity—see everything through the lens of our own temperament, early conditioning, brain function, role and place in society, education, our personal needs, and our unique cultural biases and assumptions."[192]   As this work repeatedly states, the personality tool is simply a method to help one assess weakness and choose personalized practices for on-going transformation.

Disciplines are vital because they anchor a person in habit; and habit is the place where character is forged. In James K.A. Smith's work, *Desiring the Kingdom*, he focuses on this missing reality in most congregations:

> Human persons are intentional creatures whose fundamental way of "intending" the world is love or desire. This love or desire—which is unconscious or noncognitive—is always aimed at some vision of the good life, some particular articulation of the kingdom. What primes us to be so oriented—and act accordingly—is a set of habits or dispositions that are formed in us through affective, bodily

191 Maitri, *The Spiritual Dimension of the Enneagram*, loc 4753.
192 Richard Rohr, *Eager to Love: The Alternative Way of Francis of Assisi* (Cincinnati, OH: Franciscan Media, 2014), 3.

means, especially bodily practices, routines, or rituals that grab hold of our hearts through our imagination, which is closely linked to our bodily senses.[193]

One of the ways to experience the power of God is through intentional practices that routinely place the worshiper consciously before the presence of God. God alone, then, has the power to transform humans from within. Thomas of Kempen, the medieval mystic, understood this concept when writing his seminal work, *The Imitation of Christ*: "If thou rest more upon thy own reason or experience than upon the power of Jesus Christ, thy light shall come slowly and hardly; for God willeth us to be perfectly subject unto Himself, and all our reason to be exalted by abundant love towards Him."[194]

Therefore, practices are ways that humans can initiate contact with God, yet surrender to God within the discipline, in order to be transformed by grace. A simple example of this is Bible reading. One must actively open the Bible, yet must passively be transformed through permitting God to reveal, convict and restore when exposed to biblical truth. Humans are active to pursue, yet are passive in receiving power for transformative purposes. Therefore, spiritual disciplines are not just willful piety of human effort, but willing practices where God makes contact.

The Enneagram imparts knowledge of self. Practices invite participation with God. For one to assess their Ennea-type and then engage in practices is a pathway to transformation.[195] The following contents specify two practices to challenge each Type. The first is referred to as "downstream." This means that this practice will come easily to the Type as a result of personality and Triad. It is encouraged for the participant to continue this practice. The second is "upstream." This practice will most likely not come easy to the Type. However, it is necessary because the prescribed discipline will challenge the weakness of each Type. Upstream disciplines

---

193 Smith, *Desiring the Kingdom*, 62-63.
194 Thomas à Kempis, *The Imitation of Christ (Illustrated)* (London: Penguin Publishing, 2006) Kindle Edition, 13.
195 Riso, *The Wisdom of the Enneagram*, 343.

are critical because these are the practices each type seeks to avoid. In avoiding upstream disciplines, disciples evade transformation. Brooks rightly states,

> Character is built in the course of your inner confrontation. Character is a set of dispositions, desires, and habits that are slowly engraved during the struggle against your own weakness. You become more disciplined, considerate, and loving through a thousand small acts of self-control, sharing, service, friendship, and refined enjoyment. If you make disciplined, caring choices, you are slowly engraving certain tendencies into your mind.[196]

Confronting oneself is vital to transformation. The Enneagram imparts information of where confrontation is most needed. These areas should not be ignored, but explored. Riso believes, "To climb the levels of development toward integration always requires a struggle against everything that draws us downward."[197] Practically, winemakers testify that the best wine is created only after grapes struggle. In other words, they must suffer. The taste of good wine derives from struggle and suffering, transformed into something new and enjoyable for others. This viticultural truth also applies to the formation of the human life. When one experiences a kind, loving and wise person, rest assured that person has toiled in his inner life to form a generous character, depth and charity over a long period of time through specific practices.

At the conclusion of each Type, a season of the Church calendar will be recommended as the most important time of year for the congregant. This is due to differences in personality. In congruence with the order of Triads (Chapter 3) and biblical narratives (Chapter 4), the list will begin with the body Triad and proceed clockwise.

---

196 Brooks, *The Road to Character*, 263-264.
197 Riso, *Enneagram Transformations*, 24.

Type Eight

Eights are justice oriented. The downstream practice for this Type is to commit to regular opportunities to contend for the common good. This can take various paths such as serving weekly in a local soup kitchen, advancing a cause that is worthwhile or raising funds for the underprivileged deprived of water, resources or medical supplies. Eights naturally come to the rescue of others and are not afraid to get involved. Although they are sometimes perceived as aggressive, healthy Eights are aggressive toward causes they most believe in.

The upstream discipline Eights need is accountability from others around them they trust. This Type often avoids vulnerability. They often are unaware of how others perceive them. For an Eight to move toward holistic transformation, inviting others to provide feedback about their life and conduct is essential. Connecting with a small group in the local church or regularly pursuing open conversation with trusted friends must be intentionally sought or it will most likely never occur. Trusted friends are there to love in truth. This may be difficult because Eights can be intimidating, thus others will rarely freely provide the feedback they most need. This Type needs to seek out others, invite their honesty and humbly receive their feedback. The writer of Proverbs believes, "Wounds from a friend can be trusted" (Prv 27:6). Trusted friends smooth out one's jagged edges.

The season in the Church calendar Eights should engage most intentionally is Pentecost. This season serves to remind that God cares about justice even more than they do. The Scriptures purport that God is making all things new (Rv 21:5). Partnering with God relieves the heavy load of individually carrying justice in the world. This posture can also instruct Eights to hold justice without always demonizing opponents. Believing God will have the final word in every situation can assist this Type to fight for justice, submit to God and rest that all will, in time, be put to rights. Therefore, as Eights engage the world with the hope of justice, their prayer becomes, "Come, Lord Jesus."

Type Nine

Whereas the vice of the Nine is sloth, the virtue is action. Therefore, it is helpful to think of transformation for the Type in terms of engagement and conviction. The downstream practice for the Nine that will come easy is time in nature. Walking nature paths, hiking or climbing, strolls along the beach and running in parks aid the Nine in restoring balance. Nature also serves as a calming practice in the midst of all the details of life. Nature is often restful for the Nine, and helps them return to life with peace and calm. Nines are often in the middle of conflict, operating as intermediaries between conflicted parties. Nature reminds them that life does have order despite its complexities.

The upstream practice for this Type is fixed hour prayer. Jesus entered a Jewish context where the community oriented life around three specific times of prayer—morning, noon and evening. The early Church followed the formation of the *Didache*. This formation manual prescribed Christians to also pray three times daily.[198] Since that time, many variations of fixed hour prayer have emerged. The Trappist Monks are perhaps the most rigorous community oriented around prayer. This monastic order even rises throughout the night to pray. Often referred to as "The Liturgy of the Hours," fixed hour prayer can be helpful to a Nine because it prioritizes God's presence and seeking God's wisdom and guidance amidst the hustle of life. Whereas many do not feel the call to rise and pray frequently throughout the night, it is advised to follow the early Christian formation plan to stop three times per day to re-center toward God. Upon waking up, before lunch and prior to bed are three natural times to pray. In movements such as the Benedictines (named after St. Benedict who founded a monastic order in Monte Cassino, Italy), these three times of prayer are referred to as *lauds* (morning prayer), *diurnum* (noon prayer) and *compline* (night prayer). The priority of prayer is challenging to Nines who often get confused about what matters most within a calendar of activities and responsibilities. It

---

198   Adele A. Calhoun, *Spiritual Disciplines Handbook: Practices that Transform Us* (Colorado, Springs, CO: InterVarsity Press), Kindle Edition, loc 224.

may also be helpful for this Type to consider meeting regularly with a spiritual director who can assist discerning life decisions.

The church calendar season Nines should heed is Epiphany. Beginning with the arrival of the Magi at the manger of Jesus, Epiphany reminds the Church of her vocation to face outward toward the other, to share the Light of Christ. This season in the calendar challenges this Type to be bold in using their voice. Nines are rarely in danger of over-exerting and over-vocalizing. Therefore, being bold to use their voice is instructive and formational for them. Due to their longing for peace and restoration, Nines can remain silent in hopes to avoid conflict. However, lasting peace and restoration has been made available through the cross and resurrection of Christ. Sharing this good news with others is the meaning of Epiphany and good medicine for the Nine.

Type One

The vice of Type One is anger, and the virtue is serenity. Practices, therefore, should be selected with this trajectory of transformation in mind. Like Type Nine, the One also finds nature walks helpful as a downstream practice. Not only does nature rejuvenate a weary soul, but it removes any temptation to judge and critique oneself. The focus during the walk is taken away from the self and put onto something grander, wilder and beyond control. Seeing God in nature can restore a One and calm any brooding anger underneath. Although one's inner world may not be perfect, God's promise is to perfect all in due time. Nature reminds them of God's power and beauty to do this.

The upstream discipline for Type One is journaling. The trouble with journaling is the honest confession that occurs on paper. To articulate imperfection is difficult, but to record imperfection on paper can be emotionally painful. When one writes out the cries of the heart it can feel more official and truer than if it remains in the head. Therefore, it is easy to understand why journaling would be difficult. However, there is another facet to journaling that is hopeful for the One. When one records the details of life (the good, the bad and the ugly) it can provide a sense of understanding the whole. Some refer to this as a kind of "altitude" where distance is created for the sake of perspective. Putting life's complexities into perspective can be resourceful as the One is prone to feeling overwhelmed. Journaling helps to get the issues of life onto paper so they can be previewed and understood rather than subconscious and emotionally heavy. When journaling, this Type should not only focus on the challenges, imperfections and tensions of life, but also on what is good and what is working in life. Celebration and thanksgiving are key components for the One for ongoing transformation.

The day in the Church calendar that Type Ones should focus on is Good Friday. This is a painful day in the course of the Christian year. In fact, it is the most painful day recorded in human history according the Christian tradition. On this day, God bore the sin of the world through Jesus' death on the cross. Ones should mark this as the annual reminder that "he was wounded for our transgressions, crushed for our iniquities; upon him was the punishment that made us whole, and by his bruises we are healed" (Is 53:5 NRSV). This means that all imperfections were put on Jesus, the perfect one. In the Western Church there is a liturgical expression for Good Friday called *Tenebrae* that serves as a meaningful way to observe the cross event. At this service, candles are snuffed after sequential readings of the crucifixion account. After the last candle is snuffed, the congregation leaves in silence, remembering the significance of Jesus' death. Type Ones are often struck with how significant the service is because it reminds them that they do not have to carry their imperfections alone. They can give them to God and trust his eternal plan and his commitment to the process of maturity.

Type Two

Type Twos are paradoxes. Whereas they are often the greatest servants, their vice is pride. A healthy and transformed Two will walk in deep humility. Disciplines should be selected with both the vice and virtue in mind. The downstream discipline of the Two is hospitality. Twos know how to bless others. Opening their homes, hearts and pocket books comes easily to them. The key to a transformed Two is serving as an end and not a means. Healthy Twos do not serve out of compulsion but conviction. Transformed Twos give because they want to and not because they have to. They also serve and give without any expectations or *quid pro quos*. Hospitality is a godly ambition when Twos operate from a place of health (Rom 12:13, 1 Tm 3:2, Ti 1:8, 1 Pt 4:9, Heb 13:2). This can take the form of hosting dinners for guests, serving on mission trips, contributing to a local project, serving as a deacon/ness or simply being available to others in a time of need. Creating a monthly dinner for friends, acquaintances or strangers is a helpful rhythm and discipline in the Western context. This Type should practice not expecting anyone to return the favor or contribute. This trains the Two to serve without any expectation.

The upstream practice of the Two is centering prayer. This form of prayer has been utilized throughout the centuries, but was revitalized in recent decades by Father Thomas Keating, a Trappist Monk in Snowmass, Colorado. Centering prayer is a form of stillness that invites being over doing. This form of prayer demands the disciple to simply show up before God and relent any performance, action or doing. Novitiates to intermediaries of this practice often will connect their breathing with a word. This word stunts the frontal lobe of the brain and helps one to become still, listen and sit before God. Solitude can be a struggle with restive Twos because it is like an existential look in the mirror. Centering prayer resides in the *apophatic* mode of spirituality. Apophatic spirituality is accessed through negation or unknowing. The aim in apophatic spirituality is not acquiring, information or acquisition. Rather, it is slowing, being and resting with God. It connotes addition by subtraction, which is a lost pathway in much of the Western Church. To explore more on this pathway, Keating's seminal work, *Open Heart, Open Mind* is a helpful resource to begin the journey.

The day in the Church calendar that Twos should heed is Maundy Thursday. *Maundy* is derivative from the Latin, *Mandatum*, which means command. The command Jesus gave during the supper was to love one another. Illustratively, he demonstrated this by washing the disciples' feet. Peter resisted, and Jesus informed him, "Unless I wash you, you have no part in me" (Jn 13:8). Twos are more comfortable doing the washing. This day requires that they be served rather than serve. Their vice of pride will cause them to want to resist. Humility must lead them beyond that temptation to receive the washing.

Type Three

Spiritual disciplines that confront deceit and yield authenticity are valuable for Threes. A preoccupation with image and perception prevent this Type from accessing their true selves. This explains why they often are out of touch with self-awareness. The downstream practices for this Type can be anything *kataphatic* (also spelled *cataphatic*). This mode of spirituality connotes affirmation and acquisition. Practices like Bible study, reading groups and spiritual courses are helpful for *kataphatic* learners. For Type Three, a 365-day Bible reading plan is beneficial. Naturally, a plan will appeal to their sense of goal-orientation and present the opportunity for accomplishment. These kinds of plans inspire this Type to achieve a desirable outcome.

The upstream practice that will challenge the Three is confession. Confession requires the disciple to get in touch with what is under the surface. Threes hide from authenticity as a strategy to protect their image in the world. Whereas some church traditions celebrate and offer formal processes of confession, this practice has declined immensely in the last few centuries. This is partly due to a rise in individualism and private spirituality. However, one should not neglect the Scripture that implores the Church to "confess sin to one another" (Jas 5:16). Whether the Three confesses to a priest, a friend or a group of believers, it is vital this practice becomes operative. Confession requires self-examination, emotional connection and then humble repentance for things done and left undone. Riso believes, "Change and transformation do not—and cannot—occur without emotional transformation."[199]   Although confession is demanding, the practice invites this Type to move from self-deceit to authenticity. From his interpretation of the *Philokalia*, a collection of teachings from the Desert Fathers, Anthony Coniaris submits, "To be spiritual is to be in the process of becoming a new creation in Christ."[200]   Similar to Ones, Threes have to make peace with the journey—that they do not have to be perfect and project the illusion of competence in all things.

Other recommendations for this Type include frequent fasts from social media, which forfeit public displays of perception. According the woes of the Pharisees in Matthew 23, one of the things Jesus despises most is externalism. Threes have to work at ridding themselves of pretense and striving to control the way others perceive them. Essentially, Threes live in the purgatory of meritocracy. Liturgy comes easy for Threes, but emotional processing and stillness prayer are hard work. Lent is a good season for Threes to practice, but the day in the Church calendar that Threes should pay most attention to is Ash Wednesday. This day invokes sobriety that all will die. It calls the Church to survey the meaning of pursuits and achievements, and then to adjust where there are meaningless pursuits that promote vanity. Transformation is a difficult journey for all, but it is especially difficult for Threes because they must surrender illusion and face reality.

Type Four

Fours wrestle with envy and must strive for emotional balance. Practices should be chosen in view of this pathway to transformation. The downstream practices that come easily to Fours include solitude and journaling. Solitude provides them space to dream, imagine and think creatively. Without solitude, Fours feel dry. Journaling offers them pages to explore life, its meaning and to release the swirl of the inner monologue. Fours enjoy praying

199   Riso, *The Wisdom of the Enneagram*, 360.
200   Anthony M. Coniaris, trans., *Philokalia: The Bible of Orthodox Spirituality* (Lakeland, FL: Light & Life Publishing Company, 1998), Kindle edition, locs 1098-1099.

through journaling. This Type should aim to intercede for others when in solitude and when journaling to avoid self-preoccupation. Often this self-preoccupation can lead to arrogance if life is going well or depression if it is not. Exclusive self-focus is what the Four will want to avoid in solitude and journaling.

The upstream practice that Fours need, but will aim to avoid is feasting. Feasting should not only be viewed as a time to eat, drink and be merry, but also bear in mind a specific people with whom one can cultivate joy, peace and thanksgiving. Speaking out what one is thankful for while feasting opens the community to experiencing joy and celebration together. Joy spawns more joy. This practice will help the Four get out of himself and also will force him away from extreme melancholy. Fours should schedule regular feasting with consistent people they know and trust. Many Fours espouse the need for practices that require structure while also submitting to a regimented sleeping schedule.

The day in the Church calendar that is most important to Fours is Easter. This day is one long celebration that Light has come, and that death has not overcome despite the darkness of Good Friday. Many Fours can mask their darkness while appearing to be in light. Easter is hopeful for them that no matter how dark their inner world may at times be, joy comes in the morning, and there will be a day when that morning light will remain forever. These practices and times in the annual cycle will assist the transformation of a Four moving from envy to emotional balance.

Type Five

Fives are in a battle with greed and must move toward non-attachment. Although their greed may be monetary, often it is greed for knowledge. They seldom share their insight unless asked and feel no compulsion to assert their voice. Many Fives are content to hoard their knowledge and do not seek validation from others. They do not realize that what they know can bless others if they would share it. The downstream practice for this Type is inductive Bible study. This method of Scripture reading engages the mind while fostering a sense of growth toward God. For example, a word in original language or an understanding of God's character can deeply move Fives. Reading books on various subject matter is also a helpful practice for the Five.

The upstream discipline Fives find difficult is regular service projects. Fives should aim to get out of their heads and engage their hands. Committing to a consistent mission such as Habitat for Humanity, a soup kitchen or any regular activity that involves serving other people will challenge the Five. They prefer to remain in their headspace and acquire information. The shema (Dt 6:4) in the Hebrew Bible reminds the disciple that humans are made to worship God with their whole selves and not just the mind. Engaging the body is necessary for the ongoing transformation of this Type. When serving others, Fives are reminded that knowledge can be attained through the hand as well as the head.

The season Fives should pay close attention to is Christmastide. These days are marked as the twelve days of Christmas where the Church celebrates the arrival of Messiah. Because Fives are committed intellectuals, they can become argumentative and cynical. Further, they are prone to live in the world of theory and concepts rather than pragmatism and materialism. Christmas is a necessary season for them because it brings them back to flesh—to incarnation. The eternal Son of God was enfleshed in a body. Spirituality is both cerebral and carnal. Fives must reject a spiritual-material divide and develop a sacramental imagination that physical matter matters to God. The twelve days of Christmas immerse Christians in this truth.

Type Six

The vice of Type Six is fear. Transformative practices will move this Type from fear to courage. Singing and journaling are natural practices for this Type. Singing reminds Sixes of the truth they can claim. Singing with others solidifies they are not alone in their convictions. Journaling aids a Six to feel safer when the fears of life are listed in front them. It is a way to feel like they have some control or mastery over situations even if they do not. The downstream practice that Sixes should commit is a specific way of reading Scripture—*lectio divina* (Latin for "divine reading"). In the sixth century Benedict developed this meditative approach to Scripture reading. The method prioritizes what God is speaking today as much as what God spoke in ages ago. *Lectio Divina* invites the Holy Spirit into the reading as it moves the reader in four distinct directions after a text is selected: read, meditate, pray and contemplate. The benefit of this way of Scripture reading for the Six is to provide a mix of *kataphatic* and *apophatic*. The reader is able to discern Scripture, which builds conviction and courage. Yet, this way of Scripture reading invites the disciple to rest at the end. For a Six steeped in fear around various facets of life, this practice is essential and natural.

The upstream practice for this Type is Scripture memory. To be sure, Scripture memory is an antiquated discipline that most find difficult in a world of sound bites, social media and over-stimulation. The reason Scripture memory can assist the Six in transformation is because it anchors the disciple to commit Scripture beyond reading. This means that wherever they go and whatever they face, Scripture has been sown into their soul and they can recall it in times of trouble and anxiety. It is advised the Scriptures are chosen which remind the person of hope and courage in times of fear and disappointment. For example, when facing a seemingly insurmountable circumstance, recalling Joshua's commission to "be strong and courageous" is meaningful. Furthermore, Scripture memory calls the disciple to submit to the authority of Scripture, grounding them in objective reality beyond their circumstantial moment. This can serve as a safe refuge amidst a tumult of confusion and transience.

The season in the Church calendar that Sixes should fully embrace is Advent. Advent is the reminder that darkness will not win and that Light is on the way. The incarnation teaches the Church that fear will never have the last word. Sixes would do well to heed this time of year and live in the tension of the "now" of God's Kingdom and the "not yet." This perspective does not eradicate worst-case scenarios playing out, but it does provide hope that whatever transpires is within God's sovereign purpose, and will work together for good.

Type Seven

The transformation of Sevens is the invitation to move from gluttony to sobriety. In the twenty-first century, the term gluttony conjures nearly exclusive imagery of American obesity. Whereas this is a form of gluttony, the term extends beyond the waistline. Excess has become a Western value. Americans "supersize" everything—burgers, alcohol, credit cards and entertainment, such as "binge watching" television shows over the course of an entire weekend. Sevens are particularly prone to excess in various areas of life. Practices should be selected with in mind. The recommended downstream practice of the Seven is feasting. Many Sevens are gregarious, extraverted and exciting to be around. They feed off energy and seldom shy away from the center of a moment. Feasting gives them reason to enjoy life with others. When Sevens practice feasting they should connect it with purpose, such as meaningful conversations that develop relationship or prayer with others. When they feast, this Type should keep the propensity of excess in mind to ensure they do not over-indulge in any way (eating and drinking for example). They must also remember that Scripture calls the body the temple of the Holy Spirit (1 Cor 6:19). Secondly, Sevens must not exploit feasting to avoid their inner life. Cultivating a robust inner life yields greater meaning when feasting with others. When a Seven ceases to pursue others when feasting, and merely seeks attention for her/himself, it should serve as a clue that self-love is most likely at the center.

The upstream practice for this Type is solitude and silence for a specified period of time each day. Sevens must discipline their lives to look within. Solitude releases them from performance with others. Silence reminds them of the quiet whisper of the Spirit within in, which serves to counsel, convict and intercede (Rom 8:26-27). Sevens should set aside time each day that is sacred for solitude and silence. Mornings, before the rush of the day begins, is a good time for this practice. It serves as a reminder that their identities are not based on how others feel about them, nor on how they feel about themselves. Rather, they can recall God's pronouncement of their belovedness and live from that place.

The time in the Church calendar this Type should heed is Lent. Lent is a forty-day period of self-reflection, sobriety and self-control. Beginning with Ash Wednesday, Lent informs followers of Jesus that they will die and are living in a spiritual battle. Just as Jesus went into the desert for forty days before beginning his public ministry, so they too follow Jesus into the desert of their inner lives, to discern where growth is urgent. During this season, another practice that is helpful and challenging to Sevens is fasting. Fasting instills dependency on God for all things, reminding followers of their true longings. Jesus once said that man does not live by bread alone, but by the words that come from God's mouth (Mt 4:4). Fasting invites the disciple to say "no" to good things in order to say "yes" to the best thing.

6

CONTEXTUAL SUMMARY
AND CONCLUSION

Enneagram in Church Context

Scaling the Enneagram from personal use to a local church context can be challenging for many reasons. The first challenge is awareness. Many congregations are unfamiliar with the personality theory. The second challenge is credibility. Chapter 1 detailed varied suspicions (and responses) some have to the Enneagram. Another challenge is identification of Type. The second chapter of this work attempts to consolidate each Type for the purpose of quick identification. The purpose of this is to quickly assess so that one can move into practices that transform.

As previously stated, the Enneagram is a means, not an end. The information from the Enneagram imparts self-awareness to lead one into deeper Christ-like formation. A fourth challenge, specific to the Enneagram, is sorrow. For some, the Enneagram is very painful because of the weaknesses it reveals. This is especially true for those who tend toward unhealth in their personality. Some avoid the Enneagram altogether out of fear of despair. However, because of the hope of transformation through practices, one need not relate to it this way. The Enneagram can be a tool of help despite how devastating it may be. Whatever challenges surface in congregational use, the invitation past the theory into personal and communal practices can assuage fear.

At Trinity Grace Church Chelsea, a parish in Manhattan, the Enneagram was first introduced on December 8, 2015. Partnering with author and Enneagram practitioner, Scandrette, the staff developed a two-week workshop to help the congregation quickly and effectively discern Type, and then led them into selecting practices in week two. Around 150 parishioners attended the workshop. From the workshop a focus group was created for ongoing learning and discussion.

After the first meeting on Thursday, January 28, 2016, the group was further categorized to continue meeting based on Triad. Each Triad met independently to discuss a wide range of spiritual practices, and discern practices that came easily, and also those with difficulty. They then selected practices to commit to over the season of Lent. Results came back varied. Most had an incredible journey of self-discovery, pairing specific practices based on personality. However, a few found the journey far too difficult due to the demands of New York life with regards to time and capacity. This should be anticipated as normative.

Transformation becomes plausible only after one assesses their Type, commits to practices that challenge the various personalities, and survey their growth over an extended period of time. One should not anticipate immediate results, as transformation bears greater similarities to agricultural phenomena as opposed to efficient production from the industrial age. The results of the focus group participants are located in Appendix L.

Within the context of the local church, there are many ways to engage the Enneagram and introduce practices toward transformation. Trinity Grace Church Chelsea will hold the same two-week workshop each Autumn before Advent. The first week will be instructive to assist participants to assess their Type. Chapters 1 through 3 of this resource will be the required reading material prior to attending week one. On week two participants will be grouped based on their Type. Chapters 4 and 5 will prove instructive to locate a biblical narrative of each Type and then recommendations of spiritual practices. Groups will discuss their reactions to the practices and then individually develop a path toward routinizing spiritual disciplines through the upcoming season of Advent. A retreat will be designed each Lent as a weekend to provide feedback and learning lessons amongst the group. Results will be recorded and improvements made for the annual Autumn workshop.

Conclusion

The potential impact of the Enneagram as a self-awareness tool for formation is significant. First, the Enneagram affirms human diversity. As nine "faces of the soul," the personality theory reveals a robust approach to spiritual formation as both necessary and imperative in the local church. Second, the self-revelation it provides for increased self-awareness opens the disciple toward analogous biblical narratives, spiritual practices and key moments in the Church calendar for ongoing character formation. Kathryn, a participant in the Trinity Grace Church Chelsea focus group, testified to impact of the Enneagram in her life only one month after the first workshop:

Thank you again for letting me participate in the Enneagram workshops and focus group. Truly, I have to say that it has been one of the greatest blessings learning about the Enneagram. I am in awe with the work God is doing on my heart, and how much self-awareness has come from this.

As a two, I feel my whole heart in life is to love and to give to others. Yet, I find it difficult to receive love back. After reading the fears of the Two, I was able to confirm my Type. Since the day my father left our family, I've prayed for forgiveness and tried to reach out. Thus far he is disinterested to reconnect. This breaks my heart and has spawned my deepest fears—that I'm unlovable and not worthwhile. It has carried into my other relationships, especially romantic ones, which has made me so sad. I no longer seek to be so scared and distrusting.

I simply want to reach out to let you know how special, hard, and sanctifying this learning has been for me. I know I'm only just begging to chip away at the tip of the iceberg here, but already I feel God opening my heart to receive more His love, and the practice of contemplative prayer has helped me in this season. God is quieting my soul and helping me to realize that I am worthy of love and that not everyone will leave as my earthly father has.

The Enneagram, paired with spiritual practices, can provide healing for the local church. It would be a significant mistake to prescribe bland practices that may or may not apply spiritual salve needed to repair and transform Kathryn's wounds.

Discipleship in a globalized, post-modern society is complex. Heterogeneity, personality and other contributing factors such as disparate worldviews about truth, time and transience, have increased the complexity of formation. Therefore, the Enneagram serves as a helpful tool for self-awareness. This self-awareness provides critical insight for spiritual practices that shape the follower of Jesus into his image. Although the Enneagram has contentious origins, the theory need not be demonized simply because it may not have arisen from Christian thinkers. At the same time, many suggest the Enneagram did originate from Christians. Whatever the case may be, its usefulness is not contingent on its origins since all truth belongs to God, and it should be utilized as a means and not an end.

The Enneagram is a tool best utilized for spiritual formation. As an end, it can be devastating because it tends to reveal flaws and unhealth in ways that most are unaware of prior to assessment. As a means, it can be fruitful to reveal how people grow toward health through specific spiritual practices based on Type. Kim, a participant in the January 2016 focus group at Trinity Grace Church Chelsea had a breakthrough realization: "Something clicked when I realized my tendencies are not my identity. For the longest time I thought I was just odd. So my tendencies because of who I am, which spawned a lot of self-accusation. Then I met other Fours who experienced the same things. I feel like I am resting more because of this normalizing of my tendencies. I no longer feel all alone."

Lisa, Type Four, remarked similarly in her reflections: "Initially, seeing my unhealthy and sinful patterns clearly was really painful. I'm particularly prone to the 'something is uniquely and terribly wrong with me' narrative and to ruminating on it. I was eager to learn ways to respond differently so I signed up for the focus group." To illustrate Lisa's growth utilizing the Enneagram in a life scenario, she writes:

A friend invited me out dancing to celebrate her birth-

106

day. I noticed myself falling into the "I feel out of place and different" narrative. Often, I'd fixate on this thought and the associated feelings. Usually the result is that I spend the night uncomfortable and increasingly miserable, withdrawing from those around me. Instead I noticed the thought, recognized the pattern, chose to be present, and didn't focus on how out of place I felt. Later in the evening I resolved to simply enjoy the fact that I was there with God. That quickly turned things around, and as I returned to a place of intimacy with God I actually had fun. Recently, after leaving a conversation I was reflecting on what was said and how I'd shown up in the conversation. I felt vulnerable because I thought I'd come across as awkward, a little "too" myself, too quick to speak, and too slow to listen. Often I'll nurture those emotions by texting a friend and/or cultivating self-pity through thoughts like "I'm so awkward." It's not unusual for me to get stuck in those negative emotions and feel bad for a day or two afterwards. Instead, I noticed how I was responding and turned towards God, reminding myself that he'll love and accept me even when I'm weak or awkward. And that if it was true I didn't listen well, I'll have many more opportunities to practice and learn. That was enough to get me out of my usual pattern and opened me up to worship God instead.

Many congregations are desirous to experience breakthrough in manifold ways. Given the range of personalities in any given church, reducing a pathway for limited, monolithic spiritual formation (read the Bible, pray and attend weekly services) is an ecclesiastical disservice. Personality theory takes this diversity into account and promotes various formational pathways to arrive at the same goal—Christ-likeness. To this end, Lisa from the   Trinity Grace Church Chelsea focus group writes:

Upstream and downstream practices both play key roles in spiritual formation. I was surprised to recognize that the downstream practices have supported my transformation as much as the upstream ones. I've already begun using this framework in conversations about spiritual formation. Simply recognizing that upstream and downstream practices differ from person to person is helpful. I spent most of my early days as a Christian in a community where the dominant gifts were upstream practices for me. I assumed I was just a "bad Christian" for a while because these practices came so easily to others around me.

In addition to spiritual practices, formation can take place when submitting to the annual rhythm of the Church calendar. Shiman, a focus group participant, Type Four, reports:

> Although I am not very familiar with the seasons in the Church year I think the season I should most pay attention to is Easter because it is so joyful and victorious and that is kind of the opposite of my personality. I am also interested in Ordinary Time. As a Four, the new thing for me these past years is being ordinary which is almost a fun challenge, not to make it seem like a novelty thing, but just to try to move away from the Four disposition and embrace ordinariness. I feel I'm doing a bit of that now, in really trying to carve out a devotional schedule, and most times nothing occurs to me during centering prayer but just to continue in it? I think trial and error, the process, is part of what Ordinary Time represents, really hope I'm not totally off the mark though.

Zachary, Type Three, discerned the time in the Church calendar he should most heed is, "Good Friday and Ash Wednesday (Because those times) allow me to focus on what has been done for me, and not on my performance or what I have achieved." Prior to learning the Enneagram personality theory, Shiman was unaware of how practices and various times of year play a role in her maturity. When the Enneagram is utilized as a theory toward transformation, it can reveal areas of need where growth in the Holy Spirit becomes possible.

Appendix A

Nine Personalities: "Faces of the Soul"

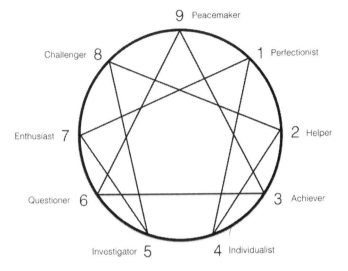

Appendix B

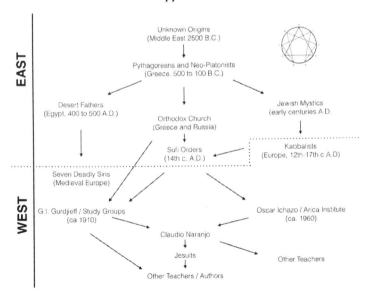

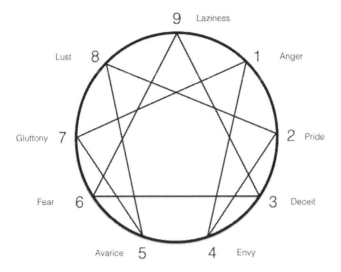

Appendix C

Roots Sins

9 Laziness
Lust 8
Anger 1
Gluttony 7
Pride 2
Fear 6
Deceit 3
Avarice 5
4 Envy

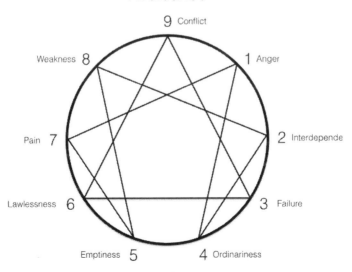

Appendix D

Avoidance

9 Conflict
Weakness 8
Anger 1
Pain 7
Interdepende 2
Lawlessness 6
Failure 3
Emptiness 5
4 Ordinariness

Appendix E

Pit Falls

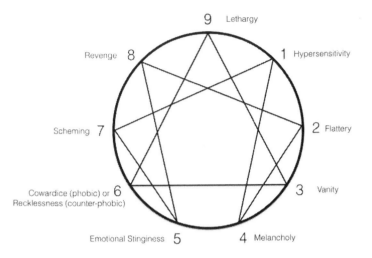

Appendix F

TRIADS: Centers

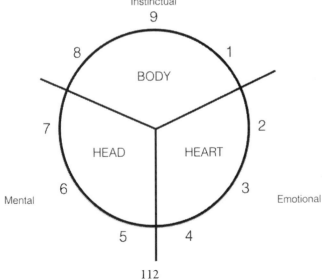

Appendix G

TRIADS: Tendencies

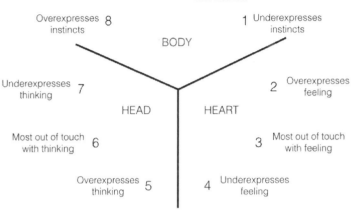

9 Most out of touch with instincts

Overexpresses 8 instincts

1 Underexpresses instincts

BODY

Underexpresses 7 thinking

2 Overexpresses feeling

HEAD   HEART

Most out of touch 6 with thinking

3 Most out of touch with feeling

Overexpresses 5 thinking

4 Underexpresses feeling

Appendix H

TRIADS: Social

Moves Against Others

9

8   1

BODY

7   2

HEAD   HEART

Moves Away From Others

6   3

Moves Toward Others

5   4

Appendix I

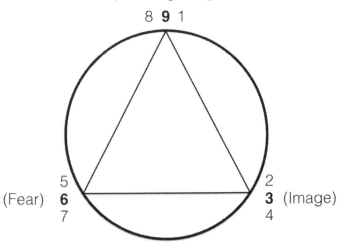

(Self-forgetting)

8 **9** 1

(Fear) **6**

5

7

2

3 (Image)

4

Appendix J

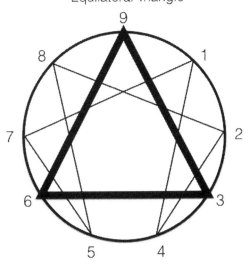

Equilateral Triangle

Appendix K

The Engle Scale

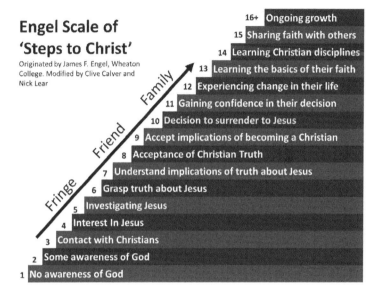

Engel Scale of 'Steps to Christ'

Originated by James F. Engel, Wheaton College. Modified by Clive Calver and Nick Lear

Family

Friend

Fringe

16+ Ongoing growth
15 Sharing faith with others
14 Learning Christian disciplines
13 Learning the basics of their faith
12 Experiencing change in their life
11 Gaining confidence in their decision
10 Decision to surrender to Jesus
9 Accept implications of becoming a Christian
8 Acceptance of Christian Truth
7 Understand implications of truth about Jesus
6 Grasp truth about Jesus
5 Investigating Jesus
4 Interest In Jesus
3 Contact with Christians
2 Some awareness of God
1 No awareness of God

Appendix L

Enneagram Focus Group, 2016

NAME	TYPE	DOWNSTREAM	UPSTREAM
Brian	2	Music Worship Focus is on God and feeling love while giving himself through song	Centering prayer because I do not like thinking about myself at all.
Katheryn	2	Music Worship because it invites hearing, beholding, responding	Contemplative prayer requires more receiving and that is a struggle.
Amy	2	Music Worship because feels connected to the people in community through song… releasing herself thru worship… singing to God is serving God… journaling prayer. Goes thru pages and pages then calls people to encourage them	Contemplative Prayer… requires me to be and not do; forced to receive and listen; make her stop and not over-process.
Craig	9	Nature walk. Restorative and calming. Things are where they should be and that brings balance. Can come back and engage with difficulty things because it feels restful.	Journaling is a difficult discipline because it's a daily task so it is on the to do list. As a 9 I want harmony, but journaling makes u address bigger issues that are easier to put aside.
Zack	3	Running, worship (things that are visceral due to triad). Anything that is an act of doing.	Contemplative prayer because it takes me out of the "driver's seat" of life and out of control and productivity. Scary but rewarding when it happens
Kim	4	Centering because she carries anxiety so centering is a relief. Day goes better when she does it	Anything that involves regiment because a lot of areas of her life are unstructured… especially since I work for myself. Going to bed at a regular time would be a huge thing for me

NAME	TYPE	DOWNSTREAM	UPSTREAM
Shaman	4	Solitude and routine such as going to bed early.	Service… Forces me to have to interact with people.
Alicia	2	Nature walks… in the world and watching people. Wing is a One because you see the harmony and you're with God	Centering… shuts out the world and lets her be in innerspace. This I find difficult
Brie	6	Worship music because you are being reminded of truths in Scripture with other people	Lectio Divina… deeper level of understanding and structure to break down scripture… Scripture memory to remind when feeling fearful/anxious
Laura	4	Journaling because it helps to define and release the swirling inner monologue. Focus when I'm trying to pray by moving my hand writing to keep from being distracted	Centering to quiet the noise
Chi	6	Anything that gets me NOT thinking… physical activity, worship	Centering prayer. Journaling is sometimes scary because it makes me confront my thoughts.
Lisa	4	Individual musical worship. I would dance in the corner. Gospel music is helpful because it cultivates joy	Meditative Prayer from Keller through the Bible. The acronym ACTS helps ground toward objective truth
Sarah	5	Disciplines I can do with others are helpful. Confronting God on my own is hard and scary. I can do all practices if held accountable and doing it with someone	Journaling. I'm good at note taking and bad at journaling. Past experiences make her suspicious to feel and to surrender to God.

NAME	TYPE	DOWNSTREAM	UPSTREAM
Haley	6	Journaling. If I get all my thoughts down they feel on paper and away from me.	Contemplative prayer. In my head so much that I need to be in places where I can rest emotionally and bodily. Letting emotions be and not thinking them out. Listening to worship music
Fredy	6	Lectio Divina and things with cerebral. Lectio Divina gives u space to do that then surrender it beyond cerebral	Concerned about outcomes so bound in indecision. Decisions are paralyzing, so I don't make the choice for fear of the outcome. Prospect of Scripture Memory helpful to have something to reflect on what God says is true. There is a promise made and I can trust it.
Rebecca	1	Nature walk - inspired by visual beauty so God's creation heals her heart. I can do the walk perfectly and there is nothing in it that I can judge myself on.	Journaling. Times when I've done it have been fruitful, but it's hard to face my own imperfections, and that is hard.
Matt	8	Anything I can do by myself. Musical worship by myself. He doesn't like to pray in community. Galleries. Anywhere I can go and be by myself… goes with a plan in mind with how he might attack the gallery… tried to do the Louvre in 4 hours. Always an element of weird competition. A walk in central park is to say "I'm going to get to that post, and then that post, then that post"	Being vulnerable in a big group; accountability and small groups with others.

NAME	TYPE	DOWNSTREAM	UPSTREAM
Eliza	3	Restful because it's a strategic advantage for the next day. Walking thru nature; intercessory prayer; worship because it's just being and allowing her to rest yet doesn't require too much reflection on herself.	Anything that requires her to confront her own emotion. I don't like reflecting on emotions thru reading scripture because then I have to work on myself and that is another thing to do. That is internal and no one is going to notice that. If I have to stop and work on myself I might shatter then be unproductive at work.
Richard	6	Acts of service	Centering prayer, lectio divina are needed because of the stress that I cope with.
Michaela	2	Journaling at night, Sending encouraging text or emails; hospitality.	Beginning the day with contemplative prayer and journaling is hard. Taking out the trash (physical service) because no one is going to notice.
Beccy	2	Anything where I can focus on the greatness of God or part of something greater and I can be shielded by the beauty of that. (Worship and nature. Both are things bigger than me)	Anytime I have to confront my own issues. Any kind of solitude is awful because it is a mirror.
Stephen	3	Anything involving being active with a clear end in mind. Going through a 365-day Bible is great because I can make progress.	Anything where I have to be still/silent is ridiculously hard. Structured prayer / liturgy is easy. Prayer that is extemporaneous us hard and uncomfortable.

Bibliography

Abbott, Anna. "A Dangerous Practice." *The Catholic World Report*. http://www.catholicworldreport.com/Item/994/a_danger-ous_practice.aspx (accessed September 10, 2015).

Almaas, A.H. *Facets of Unity: The Enneagram of Holy Ideas*. Berkeley, CA: Diamond Books, 1998.

Alter, Robert. *Genesis: Translation and Commentary*. New York: W.W. Norton, 1996.

Avrick, David Bancroft. "How Many People Move Each Year – and Who Are They?" *Melissa Data*. http://www.melissadata.com/enews/articles/0705b/1.htm (accessed November 12, 2015).

Bell, Rob. *Nooma: Noise*. http://stmartins.co.za/documents/nooma/noise.pdf (accessed November 12, 2015).

Bourgeault, Cynthia. Centering Prayer and Inner Awakening. Cambridge, MS: Cowley Publications, 2004.

Brooks, David. The Road to Character. New York: Random House, 2015.

Calhoun, Adele Ahlberg. Spiritual Disciplines Handbook: Practices that Transform Us. Downers Grove, IL: InterVarsity Press, 2005.

Coniaris, Anthony M. Philokalia: The Bible of Orthodox Spirituality. Lakeland, FL: Light & Life Publishing Company, 1998.

Flader, John. "Enneagram is not Recommended." The Catholic Leader. http://catholicleader.com.au/analysis/Ennea-gram-is-not-recommended (accessed November 12, 2015).

Gibbs, Eddie. LeadershipNext. Downers Grove, IL: Intervarsity Press, 2000.

Hurley, Kathleen V. and Theodorre Donson. Discover Your Soul Potential: Using the Enneagram to Awaken Spiritu-al Vitality. Lakewood, CO: WindWalker Press, 2000.

à Kempis, Thoma. The Imitation of Christ (Illustrated), Kindle Edition.

Maitri, Sandra. The Spiritual Dimension of the Enneagram: Nine Faces of the Soul. New York: Jeremy P. Tarcher/Putnam, 2000.

_____. The Enneagram of Passions and Virtues: Finding the Way Home. New York: J.P. Tarcher/Penguin, 2005.

Nouwen, Henri J. M. Life of the Beloved: Spiritual Living in a Secular World. New York: Crossroad, 1992.

_____. The Genesee Diary: Report from a Trappist Monastery. Garden City, NY: Doubleday, 1976.

_____. Moving from Solitude to Community to Ministry. www.leadershipjournal.net. 1995, 81.

Palmer, Helen. The Enneagram: Understanding Yourself and the Others in your Life. San Francisco: Harper, 1991.

Riso, Don Richard. Discovering your Personality Type: The New Enneagram Questionnnaire. Boston: Houghton Mifflin Co, 1995.

_____. Enneagram Transformations: Releases and Affirmations for Healing your Personality Type. Boston: Houghton Mifflin, 1993.

_____, and Russ Hudson. Personality Types: Using the Enneagram for Self-Discovery. Boston: Houghton Mifflin Harcourt, 1996.

_____, and Russ Hudson. Understanding the Enneagram: The Practical Guide to Personality Types. Boston: Houghton Mifflin Harcourt, 2000.

_____, and Russ Hudson. Wisdom of the Enneagram. Toronto: Bantam Books, 1999.

Rohr, Richard, Eager to Love: The Alternative Way of Francis of Assisi. Cincinnati, OH: Franciscan Media, 2014.

_____, Andreas Ebert and Peter Heinegg. The Enneagram: A Christian Perspective. New York: Crossroad Publishers, 2001.

Scandrette, Mark. Interview by author, August 5, 2015, New York, Phone call.

Shakespeare, William. Hamlet: A Tragedy in Five Acts. New York: S. French, 1800.

Smith, James K.A. Desiring the Kingdom: Worship, Worldview, and Cultural Formation. Grand Rapids, MI: Baker Academic, 2009.

Stabile, Suzanne. Class Lecture [discussion], Know Your Number. March 21, 2015.

Tolomeo, Diane, Remi J. De Roo and Pearl Gervais. Biblical Characters and the Enneagram: Images of Transformation. Victoria, BC: Newport Bay Publishing, 2002.

Zogby, Jon. "Employment 2.0: The Transient Age." Forbes Magazine. http://www.forbes.com/2009/09/09/temporary-employment-new-job-opinions-columnists-john-zogby.html (accessed November 12, 2015).

Zuercher, Suzanne. Enneagram Spirituality: From Compulsion to Contemplation. Notre Dame, IN: Ave Maria Press, 1992.

_____. Enneagram Companions: Growing in Relationships and Spiritual Direction. Notre Dame, IN: Ave Maria Press, 1993.

_____. Using the Enneagram in Prayer: A Contemplative Guide. Notre Dame, IN: Ave Maria Press, 2008.

25095629R00072

Made in the USA
Columbia, SC
01 September 2018